zero to something

LEADERSHIP

**This is a book about leadership.
Leading one's self. Leading a team.**

Leading a project or event. Leading an entire organization.
It's about leading in a deliberate and disciplined way.
Using a structured approach. Most of all, this book is about
results. Making progress. Moving, as the title suggests, from
zero to something.

ARNIE STREBE

WITH
JEREMIAH GARDNER

www.zerotosomething.com

Dedicated to Sigrid, my wife, for her support and
relentless resolve in helping me get this book to the finish line.

Thank you also, to my good friend Jeremiah, for contributing
his time and talents, and coaching to make the book
better than I thought possible.

Contents

CONTENTS

CONTENTS

Introduction

This is a book about leadership. Leading one's self. Leading a team. Leading a project or event. Leading an entire organization. It's about leading in a deliberate and disciplined way. Using a structured approach. Most of all, this book is about results. Making progress. Moving, as the title suggests, from zero to something.

The Fine Line Between Confidence and Humility

As a retired soldier and longtime HR and training executive, I realize this is probably the eleventy billionth leadership book on the market. I have read and prescribed many of them during my 30-some-year leadership career. *This* book, of course, is different. Better. The definitive take on leadership. The book to replace all other leadership books.

Well, not really. But such hyperbole sure sounds good, doesn't it? It's the Donald Trump School of Leadership: simply exude uber-confidence in all matters and situations, and others will surely follow … or at least buy what you're selling.

The truth, in my view, is that confidence AND humility are both cornerstones of great leadership. So, while I do passionately believe in the tenets of this book (after all, they've served me well personally), I am not naïve. No book can hold all the truths of leadership. There is no such code to be cracked. Leadership, rather, is a deeply personal and individual human affair. As such, the goal of this book is to share the leadership approach I have developed over time and, in doing so, help you start or continue on your own personal path.

In the pages that follow, you will find strategies, tactics and nuggets of wisdom that owe their origins to other people and other books. You will find even more insights based on my years of personal experience, trial and error. Most importantly, you will see how I have packaged what I learned into a framework or approach that can be internalized and applied to virtually any leadership situation.

My hope is that you can immediately apply the "Zero to Something" approach to your own leadership endeavors. As you accumulate experiences, work with mentors and develop your own personalized approach, I am confident the concepts in this book will blossom even more for you. [1]

Zero to Something – The Philosophy

The central theme of this book is results. Effective leaders, more than anything, achieve results – in themselves, in others, and in collaboration with others. They get things done by influencing destiny, rather than waiting for it to unfold. They constantly move the dial from zero to something.

So, what exactly does that mean - to move from zero to something? Well, it's a simple philosophy of constantly striving for and making progress. Not always grand progress, but progress of some kind. It's a philosophy of not sitting still, growing stale or waiting for things to happen - of having goals and breaking them down into achievable parts.

If you start at ground zero, then you should set out to move from there to anywhere other than backward. If you are already somewhere beyond ground zero, then it's important to reset the dial to zero and move from the new zero to something else. Approaching leadership with that mindset will help you to constantly make progress toward whatever ideal or ultimate goal to which you, your team, your project or your organization aspires.

The gap between ambition and reality often results because we set out to achieve too much too quickly. We are so accustomed to instant gratification that we want to achieve the end state right away. If we can't, we often ignore the ambition or abandon it quickly. Or, because we aren't willing to make gradual progress, we spin our wheels trying to "go big" and ultimately take longer to achieve our goal than we would have otherwise.

This concept really crystallized for me – not in business, but in my personal life – after I was diagnosed with ulcerative colitis (UC) in 2008. UC is a colon disease characterized by inflamed bowels, ulcers, open sores and internal bleeding. It's gross, but worst of all, it can be life-threatening. I was diagnosed only a few months after finishing my first Ironman triathlon. It was a devastating blow, not just to my health but also to my athletic lifestyle. My weight bottomed out at 129 pounds, well below my normal 165-170. Still, I carried on with training as best I could, recuperating a little day by day. Then, in the summer of 2009, I had another so-called "flare-up," with blood clotting that caused me to stop breathing. I died for a few seconds at the hospital, only to be revived with paddles in a "Code Blue" emergency. I was thankful to be alive but dejected when the doctor told me I would never be able to compete in triathlons again. Naturally, I got a new doctor!

The new doctor gave me a different story. He said I could resume my training but that I needed to be aware of the risk. Because I was on blood thinner, a bicycle crash could easily result in me bleeding to death if I were alone; I just needed to take appropriate precautions, he said. That was the news I needed! The problem was that my near-death experience zapped me. I was in no condition to race at that point, yet I was already registered for Ironman Florida just four months away. Based on my previous flare-up, I knew it was probably impossible to do the triathlon, but I trained anyway. When race week arrived, I knew for certain I would not be able to complete the triathlon So – with the encouragement of my wife Sigrid, whose caretaking and support absolutely got me through my darkest days – I decided to do the 2.4-mile swim portion and then drop out. It was not the whole shebang, but it was "something." A year later, I returned to the Florida Ironman and finished the entire race. "Zero to Something" really came to life for me during that experience.

Another trap many of us fall into is achieving and then leaving, so to speak. We reach a goal or accomplish a result, and then stop. Think some more about personal leadership away from work. Some of us set out to get married, get a job and have children. Once we've achieved those big goals, we naturally get complacent, and personal progress or further growth and achievement comes slowly, if at all. That's when it's helpful to reset the dial to zero, and set out to move from zero to something again. Improve our marriage. Get a promotion or a new job. Start a hobby. Get healthier. Volunteer. Whatever the case, lead ourselves to continual growth and progress.

We ought to do the same even when the work group we lead is well respected and earns us high praise. That's the perfect time to ask: What else can we do? Or, what can we do differently or better? Or, where do we need to be in a year, or five years? To stand pat and manage or maintain, is a recipe for later disappointment. That's why too many businesses and leaders achieve in cycles – because they don't ask those questions until circumstances necessitate it.

Again, the "Zero to Something" philosophy is to lead one's life and anything or anyone else for that matter, in a way that is filled with constant striving, growth and achievement. It

"I may not be able to do everything but I can always do something."

doesn't mean never resting, and it doesn't mean irrationally consuming oneself with getting or doing more. It simply means constantly setting out to do and achieve more of what you want in life and more of what you're capable of, at a pace that is reasonable and healthy. If, in leading yourself, for example, you envision being a master gardener, don't put it off until retirement or wait for some unrealistic "perfect" time. Be content to make gradual progress now. Go to a class. Get your soil checked. Do research online or at the big garden store. Visit a public garden and make notes about what you like and don't like. Do anything. Just don't do nothing. Go from zero to something. That's what effective leaders do. They have goals or ambitions, and they find a way to make progress.

Think of "Zero to Something" as a mindset. The mindset of always progressing from where you are at the moment (zero) to something or somewhere that brings even more fulfillment. Personally, are you learning new things? Are you improving specific things? Are you working toward specific and meaningful goals? Are you doing things today that will help you fulfill your life's aspirations? In leading others, are your followers learning new things? Improving specific things? Working toward specific and meaningful goals? Doing things today to fulfill the group's personal and collective aspirations?

Here's the secret: it's usually OK to make small progress. Let's face it - small progress is more than most people and most groups achieve on any sort of consistent basis. What's important is the consistency – constantly making progress of some kind. Zero to something. Never mind the occasional misstep. Just keep moving. If you can avoid sitting still or, worse yet, regressing backward, you will most certainly and eventually achieve. Small progress will add up to big progress sooner than you think. Ultimately, the speed with which you achieve will depend on many other factors (resources, scope of goals, number of goals, passion, team members, provided deadlines, etc.) – some controllable and some outside your sphere of influence. So, don't get preoccupied with speed. Focus instead on direction – specifically, movement in the right direction.

One of my colleagues likes to think of "Zero to Something" in terms of holiday letters. Many people are fond of writing a holiday letter on behalf of themselves and their families and sending it out to their loved ones each December. Imagine your next holiday letter now. In a sense, it is the annual report for you and your family, similar to the annual report for a business. What sort of progress will it reflect, when compared with the letter you wrote the previous year? What will you say about your own personal endeavors and those of the family members, groups, projects or organizations you lead? Will your letter reflect progress?

Sometimes, progress just happens. People and pets age, for example. Work is often handed to us, and we do what's expected. But that is not the kind of progress the "Zero to Something" philosophy aims to address. Remember, the best leaders exert influence over their destiny, rather than simply letting it unfold. So, what in your next holiday letter will reflect the influence you exerted and the progress you achieved as a result? How will it demonstrate that you are living the "Zero to Something" philosophy? Once you've sent the letter, will you reset the dial to zero, setting the stage for further progress to report in the following year's letter?

That, it turns out, is exactly the sort of thinking that represents the "Zero to Something" philosophy.

Leadership Begins in the Mirror

As I mentioned in the opening paragraph, another important aspect of this book and the "Zero to Something" philosophy is the notion that leading is leading, whether you are leading yourself, a team, a project, an event or an entire organization.

I believe people who want to lead others must first lead themselves effectively. Until we demonstrate the ability to consistently move ourselves from zero to something, we cannot effectively lead others from zero to anything. That perhaps seems obvious. Nevertheless, many people who aspire to lead often overlook the simple concept of leading one's self before others.

The fact is that many people earn leadership responsibilities by luck, birthright, force of personality, or tenure, rather than by demonstrating the ability to consistently make progress personally or otherwise.

For example, anyone can become a parent, but it doesn't mean anyone can effectively lead a family. Some folks get leadership responsibility as a reward, simply by doing what's expected of them year after year, even if they've never truly demonstrated the ability to exert influence that results in progress. Others win over decision makers with a dynamite personality or by acting the part, both of which can be good qualities, unless they mask ineffectiveness. Still others get leadership responsibilities by being in the right place at the right time.

The long and short of it is: almost anyone can get into a leadership position. But, generally speaking, only those who are truly effective achieve meaningful results and earn themselves additional opportunities. My contention is that a leader's effectiveness is often predictable, based on how effectively the individual leads herself or himself. Think of the best leaders you have encountered. Do they demonstrate effective leadership of themselves? Do they seem to have personal goals? Do they consistently make progress toward them? Do they overcome obstacles? Do they exert personal influence over the progress of their own personal health, happiness and fulfillment?

Granted, many people with personal failures have found success leading others. I'm not saying good leaders need to be perfect. Far from it. We are all flawed. I am sure you can think of many effective leaders who were divorced, demonstrated poor or questionable conduct, let themselves get out of shape, etc. Everyone has setbacks and problems. But in looking at the wide arc of people's lives, I believe it's true that those who lead themselves most effectively tend to be the ones who are most effective in leading others. Put another way, our potential for leading others can only be fulfilled by first mastering the challenge of leading ourselves; until then, we are leading at less than our full potential.

I recall the story of a former colleague who, in his first two leadership positions, earned relatively high marks from his bosses, peers and teams. But he also suffered from a substance use disorder – one that was relatively invisible during work hours but more apparent away from the office. Eventually, the disorder resulted in more problems, and the leader ended up going on leave to seek treatment. Upon his return, he opened up with his team about what had transpired, and how he was making progress. As work returned to normal, the leader eventually noted that his team seemed remarkably more committed to both him and the team's goals. As time passed, he said he felt his influence grow and that he felt prepared for additional leadership responsibility. It's easy to see why. Overcoming the illness and achieving progress personally involved setting goals, making constant progress and building confidence as a result – the kind of thing that sets an amazing example and simply makes others want to follow, whether they realize it or not. The leader's credibility grew because he demonstrated he could achieve powerful results for himself.

The most effective method of leadership is still leadership by example, and that's why leading one's self is so important to leading others. So, if you want to be a leader, are struggling in a leadership role, or simply want to be better, first look at how you are leading yourself. Are you in control of your life? Do you set goals? Learn new things? Do new things? Make consistent progress toward fulfillment?

Leadership begins in the mirror, and that is why I encourage you to apply the principles in this book not only to your work life but to your personal life as well. In fact, you ought to apply them to your personal life first!

Leadership is Practical, Not Mystical

Another key concept of "Zero to Something" is the notion of leading in a deliberate and disciplined way, using a structured approach. Now, this flies in the face of some who believe leaders are born, not developed. Or those who believe leadership is all about fiery speeches, inspiring personalities and a mystical quality – that "certain something," as they say. Qualities embodied by people such as civil rights legend Martin Luther King, Jr. or former Green Bay Packers coach Vince Lombardi.

Indeed, those are examples of incredible leaders. But I contend that their dynamic personalities represented mere icing on a cake of discipline - and that for every Vince Lombardi and Martin Luther King, Jr., there are many more relatively ordinary personalities who achieve results using practical leadership approaches.

That's why this book focuses on the practical and not the mystical. The world simply cannot wait for legendary personalities to lead. We need better leaders at all levels and in all segments of our society, which means even we ordinary folks need to lead. The good news is, we can!

The rest of this book is intended for your direct and practical application. It is basically a collection of leadership principles, each beginning with the letter R. Pretty cute, huh? Ken Blanchard, eat your heart out!

All kidding aside, there is nothing magical, or mystical,

about my 11 R's. In fact, I could probably spend some time with a thesaurus and make them the 11 T's instead. I chose R simply because my leadership approach grew originally from a military planning tool that involved documenting Rules, Roles, Relationships, Resources and desired Results. As I learned more and collected my own experiences, I gradually added to this mental template by thinking of other important leadership concepts in terms that began with the letter R. In essence, I created the R's of Leadership for the same practical reason people create mnemonics and other memory devices – so that I could easily recall and quickly reference a structured and documented way to approach, in this case, leadership problems and situations.

I also call the R's my Leadership SOPs, or Standard Operating Procedures, which I use in a deliberate and disciplined way to consistently move from zero to something in all that I do, whether at work or in my personal life.

Many leaders shy away from structured approaches – or, God forbid, building a plan – waxing on about "analysis by paralysis," "agility," "people above process" and other worthy concepts that too often are misused as excuses for lack of diligence. It is quite surprising, given the high regard for discipline shared by so many of history's great achievers and leaders.

Consider just these few examples:

"The most important single ingredient to success in athletics or life is discipline ... 1) Do what has to be done; 2) When it has to be done; 3) As well as it can be done; and...4) Do it that way all the time." – *College basketball coaching great Bobby Knight*

"The only way one can become proficient at anything is self-discipline and dedication." – *Golfing great Byron Nelson*

"Discipline is the foundation upon which all success is built. Lack of discipline inevitably leads to failure. ... It is the bridge between thought and accomplishment ... the glue that binds inspiration to achievement." – *Motivational Speaker Jim Rohn*

It's true that things rarely go according to plan, but that's no reason to avoid the practical discipline of planning. President Dwight Eisenhower once said, "In preparing for battle, I have always found that plans are useless, but planning is indispensable." In his view, and mine, leaders learn immensely from the planning process itself, equipping themselves with the

**President
Dwight Eisenhower**

knowledge needed to stay on course when circumstances inevitably change. In other words, when shit hits the fan, those who planned can dodge the poop, while those who didn't just plain stink. For the record, that's my quote, not President Eisenhower's!

Leadership SOPs

The Leadership SOPs are as follows:

1. **R**esults
2. **R**eality
3. **R**esources
4. **R**ules
5. **R**oles & Responsibilities
6. **R**espectful Relationships
7. **R**isk-taking
8. **R**elentless Resolve
9. **R**ecovery
10. **R**ecognition
11. **R**eflective Thinking

Each of the next 11 chapters is dedicated to one of the R's. By organizing the book in this fashion, my hope is to provide you with flexibility in applying the R's individually or collectively.

When taking on a new leadership assignment, for example, I find it valuable to conduct a thorough assessment using each R and to then set corresponding goals that form my plan for moving the team, project or event from zero to something. What results are currently being achieved? What results need to be achieved? What is the reality of the situation? What is the reality I need to help create? Are rules in place and if so, what are they? Which rules need to be established? Etc. You get the picture. At the end of each chapter, you will find questions that may be helpful in conducting such assessments and building your plan, or road map. You may choose to conduct assessments by interviewing team members and stakeholders. Or, to encourage forthrightness, you might enlist a third party to conduct such interviews. In still other cases, it may be appropriate to conduct the assessment based solely on observations. Regardless of your method, such an assessment will help you gain a quick awareness and understanding of "what" you need to do as a leader and "why," so you can immediately begin to think about "how" to get the job done. By participating in the assessment, your team members will gain a similar awareness and understanding of what they need to do and why, making it easier for them to contribute to discussions about how to achieve the needed results. In that sense, the assessment becomes a powerful communication tool.

I also like to apply the R's collectively when conducting an annual or semi-annual assessment, which helps me continuously reset the bar to "zero" and move toward a new "something." After having conducted an initial assessment, such follow-ups are relatively easy, requiring limited time and effort.

The R's also can be applied or referenced individually. For example, as you are faced with a particular problem, situation or opportunity, it may quickly become apparent that you need to deal with an issue involving Respectful Relationships, Recognition or some combination of R's. In dealing with that specific situation, you might reference only one of the R's, three of the R's, or all 11 of them. The nice thing is that, as you work with the R's more – and particularly after you've done at least one thorough assessment using all 11 of them – you will find it easy to recall and re-reference them individually for particular situations.

In the end, I hope you will find the book flexible enough to apply in various ways to various leadership situations. Step

#1, obviously, is to finish reading the book. In fact, if you have any urges to quit early, skip immediately to the Relentless Resolve chapter!

Reflections

Now, reflect for a moment on the key takeaways from this introductory chapter. You learned that "Zero to Something" is a philosophy, a mindset of consistently making progress toward one's ultimate goals and ideals. Small progress consistently adds up to big achievements. Our job as leaders is to exert influence on destiny. Whatever we do, we must not do nothing! Remember that leadership begins in the mirror. Lead yourself effectively, and then lead others. Remember, too, that leadership is practical, not mystical, and that discipline and structure are leadership strengths. Read on with humility but apply and personalize what you read with confidence. Your own personality and experiences are your most valuable leadership assets.

Before moving on, consider these reflective questions:

1) Who and what do you lead or aspire to lead?

2) In what ways do you demonstrate humility?

3) In what ways do you demonstrate confidence?

4) How can you balance humility and confidence more effectively?

5) What cynicisms or skepticisms do you have about leadership, leadership books or leaders themselves? How do those thoughts affect your ability to grow as a leader?

6) Who are the leaders you like to follow? Who has helped you succeed the most? Who has gotten the most out of you?

7) What about the "Zero to Something" mindset resonates with you most?

8) What do you see as your biggest opportunities as a leader?

9) How would others (i.e. spouse, friends, colleagues, employees, etc.) assess your effectiveness in leading yourself – both personally and professionally?

10) How do you assess your own effectiveness in leading yourself to personal health, happiness and fulfillment?

11) In what ways do you feel credible as a leader? In what ways do you not feel credible?

12) To what or whom do you owe your current leadership approach or philosophy?

13) What value do you see in the discipline of planning or using a structured approach to tackle problems?

14) What tools do you currently use, if any, to assess your leadership situation?

15) Why is it important to you to be an effective leader?

FOOTNOTES

[1] As you read, expect to absorb the material in three stages: 1) Awareness, 2) Understanding, and then 3) Application. These are known as the three learning levels.

Level 1 - Awareness – Upon your initial read, you will become aware of the concepts and aware of how they compare to your current leadership approach, but you may not completely understand or be able to apply them. That is normal and expected.

Level 2 - Understanding – As you get further into the book and/or begin to review it, you will start to link more of your own experiences to what you are reading, and will also start to see how the various concepts in the book relate to one other. At this level of learning, you should understand well enough to be able to teach others, even if you haven't had a chance yet, or don't know exactly how to apply what you've learned to real-world situations.

Level 3 - Application – Once you have read the book, related its concepts to your own experiences and beliefs, and reflected upon a current leadership challenge or situation that you face, it's time to take action. Do so with confidence. You have a solid foundation of awareness and understanding. You are prepared to move from zero to something in your profession and in your personal life. You are motivated to succeed. And you're ready to be a role model.

19

Results: *The consequence of a particular action, operation, or course; outcome.*

Every leader must start with the end in mind, and that is why the first **R** I will discuss in depth is *Results*.

In my job with The Schwan Food Company, I had the honor and privilege of watching a CEO who produced successful results throughout his long career. To this day, he is the most effective leader I have seen. Interestingly, I was able to work with this CEO in many capacities. First, I was an internal service provider to his business unit; then I was one of his executive coaches; then I was a peer; and finally, after he'd risen to the company's top position, I was his employee. Having seen him operate from all angles, I contend that his greatest strengths were the ability to establish a clear vision and clear goals, the patience to com-

ZERO TO SOMETHING LEADERSHIP

municate and execute on those goals until they were achieved, and the courage to constantly measure and communicate progress.

In his approach, and in my mind, achieving results involves three key components:

1) VISION and GOALS: What results do you want or need, why, and by when?
2) EXECUTION STRATEGIES and TACTICS: Who will accomplish the results, where and how?
3) MEASUREMENT: What was accomplished?

Dr. Seuss couldn't make it much simpler: What, Why, When, Who, Where, How and, for good "measure," another What.

Vision and Goals

Very little gets achieved without first setting out to achieve it, whether in your personal life or at work. Granted, some achievements may happen somewhat naturally, but they represent only a sliver of our potential. To achieve any more requires conscious decisions and effort. Remember, to lead is to influence destiny, not simply to let it unfold.

The first measure of influence is to decide WHAT it is we want or need to achieve. Put simply, we need to set a goal and write it down. The time-tested method for effectively capturing a goal is to write it down in a S.M.A.R.T. format. That is, to make it Specific, Measurable, Attainable, Relevant and Time-Bound.

Examples of non-SMART Goals

1. Complete the Ironman Triathlon
   • SPECIFIC? Could it be more specific by indicating which Ironman — Hawaii, Florida, Arizona, Wisconsin, etc.?

• MEASURABLE? Finishing is definitely measureable. If the goal-setter cares about time, he or she might want to make it even more measureable by indicating a target finish time or even the maximum finish time allowed, e.g. "within the 17-hour time limit."

• ATTAINABLE? We don't know whether this is an attainable goal. If the goal-setter has been doing shorter distance triathlons already, the Ironman may well be an attainable goal. On the other hand, if it is someone new to the sport, a more attainable goal, for now, might be to complete a sprint or Olympic distance triathlon.

• RELEVANT? Is this goal relevant to the goal-setter's ultimate aims in life? That probably depends on how much importance the person places on excellent health and/or competition, when compared with other values such as family, work, hobbies, etc. If the goal-setter simply wants to lose a little weight, one might argue that completing an Ironman is irrelevant or extra-relevant, due to the extreme commitment required; in such a case, a weight-loss goal might be more appropriate and relevant. Relevancy is difficult to write into a goal, but it's something to reflect upon when writing your own goals.

• TIME-BOUND? Finally, this goal is definitely not time-bound. By when does the goal-setter want to complete an Ironman triathlon? How much time does she have to prepare?

2. Double membership at my organization

• SPECIFIC? Depending on the type of organization, this goal could be more specific by indicating the type of membership. Family memberships? Individual? Gold level memberships? Platinum level? Etc.

• MEASUREABLE? Doubling membership is certainly measureable. However, to ensure the target is not a moving one, it may be better to indicate the exact number of memberships to which that translates, based on today's baseline. Not only would that be more measureable, but it would be more specific too.

• ATTAINABLE? We don't know whether doubling membership is attainable, partly because we don't know the baseline or the time frame in which the goal–setter seeks to achieve the goal. If it's a mature organization with an already large membership, doubling that number in a short time frame may be a stretch. On the other hand, if it's a young organization with a smaller membership, doubling may be very attainable and possibly even conservative, depending on the time frame.

1

• RELEVANT? Is this goal relevant to the goal-setter's ultimate aim or purpose at work and/ or in life? Without more information, it's difficult to tell. If the goal-setter is a membership director or head of the entire organization, and if the organization has the capacity and resources to accept a doubling of membership, then it is probably a relevant goal. If the organization is already at capacity, a more appropriate goal might be to first expand infra-structure and resources. Or, if the goal-setter's ultimate aim is to improve revenue, and if extra members will require extra resources, other goals may be more relevant to revenue growth?

• TIME-BOUND? Finally, once again, this goal is definitely not time-bound. By when does the goal-setter plan to double membership? How much time does he have to get the job done?

SMARTer Goals

1. *I will complete the 2013 Wisconsin Ironman Triathlon within the 17-hour time limit, after first having completed three shorter distance triathlons (which will be captured in separate SMART goals).*

2. *I will increase family memberships from 100 today (Jan. 1) to 200 by July 1 and will work with the operations director to ramp up resources accordingly (specifics to be captured in separate SMART goals).*

If SMART goals describe "what" results you need to achieve and "by when," then your vision helps describe "why" those results are needed. Before moving on, let me say that a lot of leaders, and employees at all levels, spin their wheels trying to sort out the difference between values, visions, imperatives, missions, and goals. Well, all of those things can serve different and important purposes but must be approached, crafted and communicated with extreme care; otherwise, they can become mere corporate mumbo jumbo, simply filling up websites and confusing more than clarifying. I will leave the lion's share of these topics to other writers (see Bibliography), focusing on the two I feel are most important: vision and goals.

I have already discussed goals, which, in the SMART format, describe specifically what you seek to accomplish in the present. A vision, on the other hand, is more future-focused. It articulates, or crystallizes, that to which you aspire, or that to which your team, project, event or organization aspires. It describes the dream of what you are trying to do and become, beyond perhaps what is possible today or ever. It describes what you want to look like in five, 10 or 20 years. It charts a course to pursue and creates a personal or organizational purpose and identity. It spells out the direction and describes the destination, informing your goals and providing a compass for all decision-making.

Vision Examples

Boeing, the great U.S. plane-making company, offers a good study in vision statements. In the 1950s, Boeing's vision statement, as cited by many writers, was "Become the dominant player in commercial aircraft and bring the world into the jet age." A relatively new company at the time, Boeing's statement guided the goals its leaders set and the decisions they made.

Often times, an effective vision statement describes an ideal for which we continually strive but never fully achieve, and that's OK. But in this case, Boeing actually did realize its vision. According to airlines-inform.com and other industry Web sites, Boeing is certainly one of the two most dominant commercial plane makers (along with Airbus), and arguably the most dominant. Along with a handful of other companies, it also deserves credit for ushering in today's jet age, where, according to the International Air Transport Association, more than 4 million people fly every day.

Having achieved its vision, Boeing had to craft a new one – one that would guide it further into the future. In 1996, Boeing adopted "Vision 2016," which remained in place at the time of this book's publishing (see boeing.com). It read: "People working together as one global enterprise for aerospace leadership." Here is how Boeing's then-Chairman and CEO Phil Condit explained the vision statement, breaking it down word by word (as captured on boeing.com):

People – A company, any company, is nothing more or less than the people who make it up.

Working – This is about effort. Work. We all have a task to do. We are here to provide value to our shareholders, to Boeing people, and to communities where we work.

Together – Every organization has forces that try to divide and reduce the impact of the total. Lockheed Martin does. Airbus does. And Boeing does. The more we can pull together, share knowledge, the stronger we will be.

One – We have a shared destiny. We will succeed or fail together. There is one Boeing stock price. This is a powerful concept. It can make us more efficient and competitive. For example, having a leak in a boat and not helping each other bail out the water is not a successful strategy. Looking for common solutions to problems, sharing facilities, sharing services, are all part of being "One."

Global – If we are to compete effectively in next century, we will be a global company. Our team will reflect global backgrounds and global experience.

Company – A company is a cohesive, inclusive institution. The dictionary uses words like "assemblage," "fellowship."

Aerospace – We are an aerospace company. We are not going to build railcars or boats. We are going to build aerospace products: airplanes, launch vehicles, satellites.

Leadership - We are not here to be also-rans. We are here to lead, to be the best, nothing less."

Can you see how an effective vision such as Boeing's provides guidance on all that a company, team, or individual does. It describes who you are and where you're going and, by doing so, should answer the question of "why" you do all that you do.

Here are examples of other corporate visions published on the Internet:

COMPANY	VISION STATEMENT
Amazon	Our vision is to be earth's most customer centric company; to build a place where people can come to find and discover anything they might want to buy online
Avon Products	To be the company that best understands and satisfies the product, service and self-fulfillment needs of women – globally
Kraft Foods	Helping people around the world eat and live better
Wal-Mart	Worldwide leader in retail
Microsoft	A personal computer in every home running Microsoft software
The Walt Disney Corp.	To make people happy
The Schwan Food Co.	A strong, solid, well-managed, fast-growing, exciting, innovative company with high business ethics and an excellent reputation – a company that offers great opportunities, a place where people like to work
Ken Blanchard Companies	To be the number one advocate in the world for human worth in organizations

1

While vision statements are most widely associated with large organizations, they are also valuable for small businesses, departments or teams within a larger organization, and even individuals.

I'm not sure where it specifically originated, but a soup kitchen vision often cited as exceptional by business leaders is: "No child in our city will go hungry to bed in the evening." Wow! That's a powerful vision.

Or, how about this vision for a local sales team within The Schwan Food Company: "Our vision is for every salesperson to qualify for the annual Chairman's Club banquet." Just so you know, that would be a rare, if not unprecedented achievement! But it's a powerful guide as to the goals you set, the people you hire, the training you conduct, the standards of accountability you uphold, etc.

Consider this individual vision, shared by a colleague of mine: "My vision is to live to age 100." My initial reaction was to say, "By then, you probably won't have any vision left!" Honestly, I'm not sure how great living to 100 sounds. But, to each his own, I suppose. For this particular individual, it wasn't so much about actually reaching 100. It was more about having that beacon for which to strive – something that guided many goals and decisions in his life regarding exercise, nutrition, health care, career choice, retirement planning, family planning, etc. The more I thought about it, I realized how powerful a vision statement it was for him, and how it answered the question of "why" he did all the things he did day to day, month to month and year to year.

What we can learn from all of these examples is that visions can and probably should be short and memorable, so that employees and stakeholders can internalize them. At the same time, it's important that every word count – that every word says something meaningful about that to which you aspire.

1

The most effective visions explain "why" you exist and "why" you are pursuing the goals you have set out to accomplish. As a leader of yourself, a team, an event, or an organization, make sure to establish a meaningful vision, stick to it, and communicate it well. Constantly remind yourself and others of the vision so as to keep the "why" in front of every stakeholder.

Bottom Line Up Front (The BLUF)

Don't stop there either. Answering "why" is such a key element of inspiring passion and getting results that, in addition to establishing a vision that articulates the big-picture "why," you also may need to frequently communicate more basic "whys."

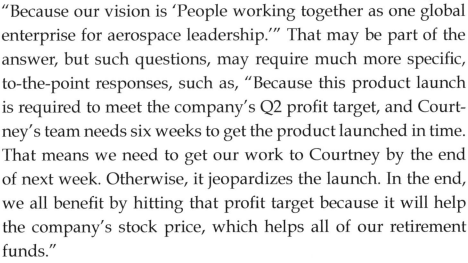

For example, a team member assigned to a task may wonder or ask, "Why is the task being undertaken and who will benefit?" It is probably ineffective to respond with, "Because our vision is 'People working together as one global enterprise for aerospace leadership.'" That may be part of the answer, but such questions, may require much more specific, to-the-point responses, such as, "Because this product launch is required to meet the company's Q2 profit target, and Courtney's team needs six weeks to get the product launched in time. That means we need to get our work to Courtney by the end of next week. Otherwise, it jeopardizes the launch. In the end, we all benefit by hitting that profit target because it will help the company's stock price, which helps all of our retirement funds."

Even better than responding to such questions is to provide

1

the answers before the questions are asked. Just assume that everybody who does work wants to know why, and provide the answer from the outset, while assigning work. I call it Bottom Line Up Front (BLUF).

Answering "why" up front may not always be easy. For example, as a leader, you may need to gather information to understand "why" you have been given a task to pass along to your team. Or, if a task falls into that "something we've always done" category, you may need to do research to determine if the task is still warranted. In other words, answering "why" up front demands that you consider "why" up front, which is a valuable discipline because it helps you identify wasteful initiatives early.

The point – regardless of scenario – is that, whenever you create and communicate goals and/or tasks to support the goals (what), it is critical to know or determine "why" you are pursuing that path and to communicate "why" to those involved in accomplishing the task. Answering "why" starts with having an effective vision that people understand, but also involves providing the BLUF whenever launching projects, assigning work, etc. Leaders and organizations that fail to answer "why" up front and instead determine or stumble upon the "why" later on, may end up misusing or wasting resources along the way.

Once you have built a vision and goals so that you and all stakeholders understand the results and why, you are ready to build a plan.

Execution Strategies and Tactics
Planning

Executing against a goal begins and ends with one thing: a plan. You have to have a plan if you are going to influence destiny and not simply let it unfold. The plan identifies how the work

1

will get done, where, and by whom. As the leader, you enable the work to get done by making sure there is a plan and that it is managed, even if you're not the one who ultimately creates and manages it.

While I have been responsible for hundreds of plans during my career, others have more thoroughly perfected the discipline of project planning and project management. I will leave you to consult them (see Bibliography) for in-depth coverage of the topic. Suffice it to say that the more important the goal (in terms of cost, risk, potential benefit, etc.), the more detailed your plan ought to be. At the most basic level, though, the plan must include the goal (what), vision (big picture 'why') and "meat and potato" details – "how" the work will get done, "where" and "by whom."

The plan should answer questions such as:

- Will the work get completed at once or will it be conducted in phases?
- How will work be handed off from one person or department to another?
- Who is going to accomplish the work?
- Who is going to plan it?
- And who is going to be responsible for supervising the action?
- Where is the work going to take place and at what level in the organization?
- Which parts of the organization will be impacted by the work?
- Do the involved parties know that they have some ownership responsibilities?

The most important thing to remember about plans is to have one. If you don't have a plan, and if you haven't built the details to support your plan, and if you don't flawlessly execute your plan, and if you don't hold yourself accountable or those you lead, then the results and recognition you deserve will never come your way.

1

Communication

A leader's greatest asset just may be the ability to communicate effectively. After all, leadership is the art of influence, and you can't influence without communicating.

As a leader, you communicate by the personal example you set. You communicate verbally – in one-on-one settings, meetings, and large gatherings. You communicate in writing – via e-mail, office memos, websites, social media and budgets. You also communicate by your policies and actions, which reflect your values and priorities, and which often signal future actions.

It is important to understand that, for better or worse, all eyes are on the leader and that everything you say, write or do is likely to be received as a communication. Even a lack of communication communicates something about you. However, when people read between the lines, they don't always "hear" an accurate message and certainly don't always "hear" the message you want them to hear. That is why it is so critical for leaders to put the highest priority on communication. A good vision, a good goal, and a good plan can produce bad results if the communication is poor.

Most human beings, you and me included, possess a natural curiosity. We want to know who our leader is as a person, what's going on, what the priorities are, why we're expected to do certain things, what to look out for, what the future may hold, etc. The more we know, and the less we wonder, the more confident, involved and engaged we feel, and the better we work as a result. Because of that reality, a leader who communicates more will almost always generate more and better results. In fact, I feel it is virtually impossible for a leader to over-communicate.

It starts with the vision and goals. As a leader, you must not only communicate the vision and goals clearly, but you must do so repeatedly. Most of us adults need to hear something at least three times before we even start to internalize it, particularly in a large organization setting. So, as a leader, be relentless about communicating "what" needs to be done and "why."

Demand even more communication from yourself and other leaders when it comes to the execution phase of a project or workflow. Success lies in the details of "who" gets the job done, "where," and, most importantly, "how." Failure to communicate here will absolutely jeopardize your ability to navigate through challenges and setbacks and ultimately will compromise your goals and results. Effective communication, on the other hand, will enable others to put your direction into action.

One communication technique I find particularly useful at all times, but especially when it comes to execution, is the **"Push and Pull"** approach. It simply means to not only "push" out the information you want to be received but to also "pull" it back from those to whom it was directed. Doing so helps you ensure that your message was heard, understood and interpreted as it was intended.

For example, once you build a plan, it is your job to make sure everyone you lead is aware of the plan, understands it, and can put it into motion with flawless execution. You do that by communicating in any variety or combination of ways – e-mail, meetings, training sessions, etc. This is the "push" part of the approach. Next, once you've pushed the message out, you need to "pull" the information back to you as a

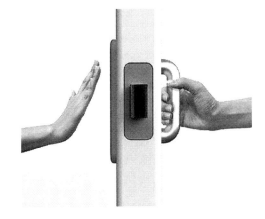

means of verifying that the recipients know and understand enough to carry out the plan. A basic method of "pulling" is simply to ask the people you are leading to tell you what needs to be accomplished, when, why, how, where and by whom. You could even ask them to put it in writing, i.e. "ink what you think." In certain situations, you may be able to stage a partial rehearsal or a role-play. Another method might be to ask the team to build and present an execution matrix back to you, or perhaps to another stakeholder, as a way of demonstrating an understanding of the plan.

I will discuss execution matrices later in this book. For now, the important thing to remember is this: Just because you sent the message does not mean it was received and understood. So, make a conscious effort to pull your messages back from the recipients. And do so all the time. Be relentless. Your messages could morph when passed from one person or group to another. You also need to become aware of challenges when they arise. So, provide people the forum to communicate back to you. The more you give, the more you will get. So, give freely. Your success depends on it.

Measurement

Now, let's discuss what makes and breaks leaders – the scoreboard! Are you winning or losing? Are you making progress or losing ground? Will you meet the goal? Then, once the game is over, "what" got done? Did you win? Are you headed to overtime? Or, is the season over? Let's face it: leaders who win lead on, and those who lose no longer lead.

Perhaps that is one reason so many neglect this very obvious area of leadership: measuring results. Admittedly, it can be a difficult task. How, for example, does a training leader or call center leader keep track of her impact on the company's bottom line? Even when you capture results, it can be difficult to *inter-pret* them. For example, what happens when a sales leader falls short of the goal but still outperforms her peers? Or, how does a sales leader who exceeds the sales goal but falls short of the profit goal compare to another who exceeds the profit goal but fails to grow sales. Or, how does a leader who exceeded goals by 5% for the fifth straight year compare with a leader who exceeded goals by 35% but fell short the previous two years?

Measurement can be tricky business. Consequently, many leaders avoid keeping track of results and evaluating them critically. It is an extension of our personal tendencies. Think of New Year's resolutions, for example. How many people keep track of progress and the final result of their resolutions? Some people may make progress without keeping score, so to speak. And some may keep score for a while but eventually stop once it becomes more difficult to put points on the board.

In the end, measurement takes some time and effort. Sometimes, it even requires creativity. It also adds pressure to achieve results. In addition, it reveals our ultimate effectiveness or lack thereof. It's no wonder it gets avoided. But it's also critical to the "Zero to Something" philosophy, which is about the disci-

1

pline of constantly making progress, resetting the baseline to zero, and making more progress. Without measurement, it's difficult to tell if you're making progress and difficult to know when it's time to reset the baseline to zero.

With all of that said, measuring results does not have to be so daunting. But it does have to be done. You just need a tool. A relatively simple, but thorough, measurement tool I've used and introduced at several organizations is the QQCT framework. QQCT stands for Quantity, Quality, Cost and Time. The premise is that leaders ought to measure their results in all four of these categories, which collectively paint a broad picture of what you have or have not achieved, rather than measuring, as we so often do, just a single number that can sometimes paint a distorted view.

Quantity – This is the use of numbers, ratios and percentages to determine whether you and your organization have been successful. What was the sales goal and the sales number you achieved, for example?

Quality – This is the use of words to describe your results and determine whether you have been successful. At the beginning of the planning process, you can put into writing what you want as the final result. Then, in the measurement stage, you can evaluate in writing whether you achieved the results originally described. This area of measurement might also capture important but difficult-to-quantify feedback from employees and customers.

Cost – This is the use of both numbers and words to specifically indicate how much a particular effort cost you, other stakeholders and the organization. Keep in mind the obvious physical costs, such as money. But also factor in what the effort cost people emotionally. You also might factor in opportunity costs and other so-called "hidden" costs. In most situations, your success will be determined by whether you were able to reduce costs or achieve results within cost limitations.

Time – How much time did it take to accomplish the result? Did you accomplish the task in the prescribed time? In many cases, success will be determined by whether you were able to reduce production, service or cycle time.

It is important that you measure against goals, not simply create measurements after-the-fact that fit the narrative you wish to portray. So, if you plan to measure in QQCT terms, I strongly suggest you set your goals in the same terms. Much of that may come naturally when you write your goals in SMART format. For example, if your goals are time-bound, it should be relatively easy to measure in terms of Time. If your goals are specific and measureable, it also should be relatively easy to measure

Quantity	Quality
Describe in Words	# Ratio %
Cost	**Time**
$	More, Less Faster, Slower

QQCT

in terms of Quantity. In my experience, however – depending on the nature of your leadership assignment – Quality and Cost do not always make it so naturally into our goals. So, my recommendation is to think about QQCT when writing your goals. It may lead you to writing separate goals regarding Cost and/or Quality, or it may lead you to weave them into other goals. Either way, it will help you to synchronize your goal-setting and measurement approaches.

Finally, I suggest finding a way to make measurement fun for you and your team. Again, keeping track adds pressure. But it also leads to elated feelings of achievement. So, do your best to make it fun. We'll talk about recognition later in the book, but as a preview, I will just say that it's important to recognize people during the pursuit of goals, not simply at the end. Encourage daily contests and games. Utilize good, old-fashioned high fives. Be creative.

It's also important to make measurement visual. The United Way, for example, encourages organizations that raise funds for it to display a fun sign depicting a giant thermometer on premises, reflecting progress as it is made each day. The premise: progress breeds more progress.

It's true. Humans tend to behave according to Newton's first law of motion. Just as an object in motion tends to stay in motion, humans or teams making progress tend to continue making progress, and those who aren't making progress tend to struggle until "acted upon by an external force." As a result, you and your team need to know at all times where you stand in terms of progress. Only then can you maintain momentum or make needed adjustments. You and your team also need to know the final score. Only then can you offer proper recognitions. Only then can you properly reflect on the process. Only then can you reset to zero and achieve results consistently.

Problem-Solving Process (The PSP)

Another "Results" tool I'd like to share - which conveniently overlays our model of setting goals, executing, and measuring - is what I simply call the Problem-Solving Process. If you are facing problems but aren't yet sure how to address them, this tool may help guide you through the process of setting relevant goals against which you can execute and measure.

Goal

1. Identify and select the problem – It is critical to identify and select the right *problem and to put it in writing from the very beginning.*

2. ***Gather and collect information and data*** *– As a leader, talk to those impacted by the problem. Also talk to experts and gather QQCT data to help you and your team solve the problem.*

3. ***Generate possible solutions*** *– This process may involve the leader and/or an entire team building possible solutions. In doing so, it's important to al ways consider what resources are and aren't available to get the job done.*

4. ***Test possible solutions*** *– If possible, do a full walk-through, or test the most viable solution(s) in a small market. If such tests aren't possible, thoroughly identify advantages and disadvantages to each solution, and select the one that provides the most opportunity for success.*

Execution

5. ***Implement solution*** *– Create an implementation plan, set it in motion, monitor progress and make changes as needed. Communicate relentlessly.*

Measurement

6. ***Evaluate your process and the solutions*** *– This is a critical step. Don't just evaluate the results of the solution using QQCT, but also evaluate the problem-solving process that led you to it. Learn from everything you lead. That way, you can duplicate what works, and eliminate or alter what doesn't.*

Reflections

Results are the driving force for all of the R's that make up the Leadership SOPs. Note I did not say that results are the end product. They are, of course. But you'll never achieve the results you want if they aren't the driving force behind all you do. Start with the results, and you will end with them!

1

As you think more about results, consider these reflective questions:

1) What process(es) do you have in place to demonstrate how you and your team add value to your organization?

2) For which results are you responsible?

3) Do the people you lead know what results they are responsible for?

4) Will your results today still be acceptable in a year?
If not, what's your plan?

5) Have you created and communicated a clear vision?

6) Have you created and communicated clear goals? Are they SMART?

7) Do you have one or more detailed plans for achieving your goals?
Do they clearly indicate how goals are to be achieved, where, and by whom?

8) Have you established methods and channels for "pulling" back the information you "push" out? What are they?

9) Do you relentlessly communicate as much as you possibly can to your team and all other stakeholders? What are your methods?

10) Are you a vision- and goal-oriented person in your own personal life? Do your work associates see that?

11) Do you provide the Bottom Line Up Front (BLUF) when assigning work so that everyone understands "why?"

12) Do you have one or more fun, visual ways of measuring progress toward goals and final results? What are they?

13) What results do you measure? Do you use the QQCT framework?

14) How do you go about finding solutions to problems? Do you wait for solutions to emerge, or do you proactively seek solutions?

Reality: *That which exists objectively, and in fact.*

We all like to kid ourselves a little bit. When you're like me – a legend in my own mind, soon to be yours – you're a little better looking in the mirror than in the eyes of others. You're a little smarter, a little more talented, a little more organized, a little more experienced, a little more grounded, a little more financially sound, a little healthier, and, yes, a little better with the ladies than anyone else would acknowledge. It's true. Just ask my wife!

The opposite can be true for those with a deflated self-image. In themselves, they see a little less than everyone else does. In either case, the lesson is the same. Our own perception of reality might not be reality at all.

This is an important notion for leaders to understand and acknowledge. It produces a level of humility that makes us question our own perceptions and seek out additional information and perspectives from others.

Reality Checks

Once we can admit that our own perceptions of reality may be biased, misinformed or lacking perspective, we are more likely to conduct "reality checks" – whether formally or informally. By balancing our own viewpoints with the perceptions of others, we generally land closer to the objective, factual reality, and we make better decisions as a result.

My awakening to this took place growing up as the son of a career U.S. Air Force airman. Like many military brats, I lived in several places all over the world. Later, while serving in the military myself, I had even more opportunities to travel. My take on reality started to switch when I saw how differently people in other countries lived. Many were less fortunate than myself, and most had relatively different outlooks on life. It was eye opening, to say the least, and made me realize that we all view life and situations from different angles and through different prisms. Because of this upbringing, I grew into an adult who was inclined to check my own reality by soliciting the views of others, and I'm thankful for that. Sometimes, what I learn confirms my own perception. Sometimes, it rounds it out. And sometimes, it stands my perception on its head. In the end, I make decisions with the confidence that I really know and understand what is happening around me – that I understand the values, beliefs and thought processes of all those who are involved and/or affected.

It sounds easy, I know. And it is. But as easy as it is to conduct a reality check, it's even easier to forget or skip. Questioning our own perception is unnatural and therefore requires conscious effort and discipline.

The Reality of Your Leadership

The ability to discern between reality and perception is paramount to your success as a leader. And it starts with understanding the reality of your own leadership. That means making a concerted effort to understand your strengths and weaknesses, not just through your own eyes but also through the eyes of others. If you don't truly know who you are as a leader, you will have blind spots that negatively affect your ability to influence others.

The key is candor. Ask yourself honest questions and give yourself honest answers. Am I leading, floating or following? Am I the leader I want to be and can be? Am I the leader I need to be to get us moving in the right direction? Change is the only constant, so if I keep doing what I'm doing now, will it be good enough in a year? Are my skills still relevant to the organization in my current position, or am I losing ground to others who are more innovative, more skilled and/or better at leading change?

Ask, too, for the perspectives of your peers, bosses, employees and friends – anyone you trust to provide an honest answer. Don't bother asking those who will suck up to you no matter what. And don't react negatively to anything anyone says,

2

Communication: The Reality of Your Leadership

or you will never get honest feedback again. Sometimes, if it's possible, it helps to have a third party collect such information and report it to you without names attached. But informal conversations can work effectively too.

The value of being real with yourself is that it puts you in the right frame of mind to lead. You lead within your limits, seek help where needed and, most importantly, begin to work on yourself professionally, which pays off immediately and in the future. By demonstrating humility, sincerity and genuineness, you also engender trust among those you lead. On the flip side, when you don't "keep it real," others see right through you.

Here's the tough part: reality isn't always what we want or expect it to be. So, be prepared. You might get surprised. And don't over-react by focusing so hard on your weaknesses that you neglect your strengths. In many cases, it's just as important, if not more so, to spend time building upon your strengths or finding new ways to leverage them. At the same time, don't ignore your weaknesses. Even if you cannot turn them all into strengths, you can find ways to minimize their impact.

Perfection is not the goal. The goal is to truly understand yourself – to be self-aware. Only then can you objectively look at how your leadership impacts the organization and its performance.

The Reality of Those You Lead

Another reality check: How capable and prepared is my team or organization? It's fun to be a cheerleader for those you lead, and that can be a proper role, but only if the cheers are warranted. If the cheers are not warranted, your energy needs to be spent on improving the team. At the same time, if you lead a group of all stars, don't withhold your cheers and go looking for opportunities to be critical just because you feel that is your role as a manager.

Once again, ask yourself tough questions and answer honestly. Am I accurately assessing those in my charge? Am I being too lenient? Am I being too critical? Are my expectations realistic? Would I want the people in my charge to lead, develop, train, mentor or coach my family members, if they applied for such a job?

Until you get real about those you lead, you will not be able to make tough decisions about them. And you won't be able to achieve the results you were hired to achieve.

The Reality of Your Company or Organization

Yet another reality check: What do I think about my employer? Do I believe in our product or service? Is the company healthy and growing? Do my values match those of the company, or do they at least not conflict? Would I recommend this company to a close friend? Could I see retiring here?

To lead most effectively, it helps to share and be passionate about your company's values and mission. It is difficult to lead when you are uncomfortable or don't "believe." So, do yourself a favor, and be honest with yourself about where you devote your talents. If you're not "drinking the Kool-Aid®," as they say, then work for change internally or make the tough, right decision to take your talents elsewhere. Just

2

don't expect to achieve your leadership potential in an environment that bores, depletes or offends you.

The Reality of Your Situation

It's also important to check the reality of your overall leadership situation. I've already mentioned the value of assessing your situation when taking on a new leadership role. I've also mentioned the value of using the Leadership SOPs as a basis for conducting annual follow-up assessments. When doing so, make sure to check the reality of each "R" you assess. Gather both facts and other perspectives, and avoid assumptions. Understand that your desired reality depends on an accurate picture of the current reality. Problems arise when you paint a picture of the desired reality but base it on an inaccurate view of today. At that point, the desired reality may be unrealistic and unachievable, and you could find yourself chasing ghosts.

If, as I suggest, you assess your overall situation using the Leadership SOPs, consider checking reality as you go by asking questions such as:

1.   Are the desired **results** realistic? Is it realistic to expect that I or we will get the job done?

2.   Am I being realistic about the **reality** check itself? In other words, am I being objective in my determinations and not biased in a way that drives pre-determined conclusions?

3.   Is it realistic to expect that we can accomplish the desired results with the **resources** available?

4.   Are the organization's **rules** realistic? Can I accomplish what I need to

accomplish professionally within the existing rules? Are my rules realistic? Can the team accomplish what it needs under those rules?

5. Are the **roles** that I am to play or fulfill realistic? Can I realistically expect those who report to me to understand and fulfill their roles? Can I realistically expect everyone who is **responsible** for action items to accomplish their jobs?

6. Are the **relationships** I have established going to realistically help me accomplish what I need to accomplish? Is it realistic to expect that the people who have to work together will do so in a healthy, supportive and **respectful** manner?

7. Am I taking realistic **risks** that push our achievements? Am I being too conservative or perhaps risking too much?

8. Is it realistic to expect that those on the project will be relentless in their pursuit of getting the job done? What may test their **resolve**?

9. Is my **recovery** plan realistic? Have I made it realistically possible for myself and others to avoid burnout and achieve optimal work/life balance?

10. Am I providing realistic **recognition** to my employees, going overboard, or perhaps expecting too much before I'm willing to offer it up?

11. Am I realistic when I do my **reflective thinking**, or do I gloss over key obstacles that impact our efforts and results?

I often recall a situation when I was in Ranger training with the Army. We trained vigorously with only the smallest amount of sleep, and one night, we were allowed to catch just a short amount of shut-eye – so short that we had to sleep in the field, in a bed of water six inches deep. Despite the conditions, it was not difficult to sleep because we were exhausted, almost to the point of disorientation. Sleep was a welcome way to escape our reality. What I remember most about that night is waking from the brief nap, wondering why it was so quiet, unaware – for the moment – where I was. When I realized that my ears were submerged in water and that only my nose and lips rose above the surface, I quickly remembered where I was, and reality set in – harshly!

In your leadership situations, don't *wait* for reality to set in. Trust me. It will be a rude awakening. Instead, be proactive. Use reality checks to *determine* what is real.

Reflections

Reality checks, are a form of reflective thinking, but they are best done early and often. Do them at any time. On any topic. As frequently as possible. Do them when you're starting a new job, re-assessing in a current role, taking over a new project, etc. All leaders should know and understand what is real and what isn't real regarding themselves, their team, their company or organization, and their specific situation. It's the only way to enable a new reality.

But keep it simple. Reality checks usually do not need to be formal or even documented. Just condition yourself to always question how honest you're being with yourself about the people and things that are most important to you and your role as a leader. Take a step back from time to time, remove yourself from the fray, and ask the reality questions. Above all else, be honest!

1) Do you seek input and opinions from others? How so? Do you allow those views to influence your perception of reality? Do you do it enough?

2) What leadership strengths and weaknesses do you possess, in your own mind? In the mind of others? How do the two compare and contrast? Are you being honest with yourself?

3) Are you leading, floating or following?

4) Are your leadership capabilities keeping up with the pace of change?

5) What do you need to do to develop into the leader you want to be and the leader your organization needs you to be? Do you have a plan?

6) Do you have the right people in the right places to achieve success for themselves and the organization? Are you being honest about their capabilities or lack thereof? What changes do you need to make?

7) Are you working for the right company or organization? Are its values and mission compatible with your own? Are you able to be passionate about your work? If not, are there changes you should be seeking to make internally, or is it time to move on?

8) When you assess your situation using the Leadership SOPs, do you make sure each of your assessments is realistic?

9) Do you determine reality, rather than wait for it to set in?

10) Have you conditioned yourself to do reality checks? Are they one of your leadership habits?

Resources: *Supplies that can be readily drawn upon when needed.*

If a leader is alone in the forest, is he really a leader? Hmm …
Probably not! At least, not until he gets out of the trees and
finds someone to lead.

Indeed, very little in this world is achieved in solitude, particularly leadership. Captains have ships, crews and passen-
gers. Political figures have advisors, supporters and campaign
war chests. Managers and coaches have teams. Leaders of all
kinds, by definition, have followers. Leaders also tend to have
budgets and deadlines, places for people, and things to use.

These are all known as resources, and they play a big role in
a leader's success or lack thereof.

Let's put it this way: If two leaders of equal capability and
equal luck compete, the one with the better resources will win.

On the other hand, a better leader can often overcome limited resources by maximizing them more. Either way, it is vital for leaders to understand how to identify, acquire, develop and utilize resources to their fullest.

Coach Wiley Wilson

Coach Wiley Wilson

I remember first thinking about resources while on the cross country team at Minot (N.D.) State University. It was a small school, and our sport wasn't exactly a big moneymaker, so we were always last to get scholarship support. Coach Wiley Wilson had his work cut out for him. He had to compete against other sports for money to recruit talented runners. At the same time, he had to compete in races against bigger schools that drew their scholarship support from a bigger pool. The odds, as they say, were stacked against him.

As it turned out, though, Coach Wilson was a more effective leader than many of his peers, and that's because he was a better resource manager. It started with his attitude. He never looked at the cup as being half empty; it was always half full. And he utilized every last drop of water in his cup, while other coaches often spilled from much fuller cups. In 30 years at the helm, Coach Wilson guided 17 conference and district championship teams in cross country and track. He also mentored 10 All-Americans and 240 individual conference and district champions. He was elected to the Minot State Hall of Fame in 1998, and when he passed away in June 2011, Coach Wilson's obituary was reported in newspapers throughout North Dakota. Pretty amazing for a small-sport coach at a small school.

Coach Wilson took advantage of walk-ons; he formed partnerships to get new track equipment; he cultivated a strong alumni network that passionately helped him recruit; he worked with students to help them manage their school/workout schedules; he pushed and challenged us; and most importantly, he treated us as something more than resources. That was the real secret to his success. He really cared. I recall when my friend and star teammate Tim Francis suffered an injury his senior year and felt guilty about it. He didn't want to disappoint Coach Wilson, so he offered to redshirt and come back for an extra year of school. Coach Wilson's response: "I can't let you put off graduation just because you think you're letting me or the team down. Don't even think of it." That's a story that Tim carries with him today. The coach cared more about him than he did his team's success. The truth is we gave him more of ourselves because of how he treated us. We all thought of him as a second dad and learned from his approach to leadership. Coach Wilson focused on the resources - time, equipment, facilities, materials, funding, and, above all, people – that he had – not the resources he didn't have. He valued his resources and got value in return.

Assessing Resources

The problem with common sense is that it's getting less common. In today's complex world, we get so caught up in the fast pace that we often overlook the obvious. So, when assessing your team, project, event or organization, do not make the mistake of overlooking your resources. Do you need more resources to achieve the desired results – now, next year or in the future? What are you willing and/or able to invest? Do you need different resources, or possibly even fewer? Do you need to develop existing resources? Or utilize them differently? Are you even aware of all the resources available? And are you getting the most out of them all?

You may find it helpful to assess your resources in terms of five categories:

Time

Do you have enough time to accomplish the objective or goal? What can you accomplish in the time provided? What are your priorities given the amount of time available?

Equipment

Is your equipment usable? Do you have the right equipment for the job? If you invested in new equipment, would it be a wise investment? Do you have access to additional or different equipment, internally or externally?

Facilities

Are the facilities adequate? Will your facilities attract the right kind of people to your team, project, event or organization? Will they attract the customers you need to be successful? Are your facilities clean, and do they present the right professional image? Are there additional or different facilities you could use, internally or externally?

People

Are the right people in the right positions? Are they inspired and motivated to get the job done? Are they being trained and developed for success? Are they being properly educated? Is their performance planned? Do they understand the rules, roles and responsibilities, and are those things clearly defined? Do they communicate often among each other, and do they communicate the right messages? Are they receiving clear, proper and frequent communication from above? Are they being recognized for their contributions? Do they have the resources they need to get the job done? Are they aware of all the resources available to them? Are they helpful to each other? Do they have support and assistance from leadership? What is your role, as leader, in all of these "people" topics, and are you fulfilling your role? Are you aware of and utilizing all available people, both internal and external to the organization?

Money

Do you have the funding needed to accomplish the objective(s) or goal(s)? Are you making the right investments at the right time?

Your MVR - Most Valuable Resource

I want to make one thing clear: of all your resources, the greatest is people! It is people, after all, who win battles and campaigns.

They're the ones who utilize the time, facilities, equipment and money. And they're the ones looking to you for leadership. So, make people your priority in all cases.

Establish clear expectations for them. Educate and train them. Give them the tools they need to succeed. Challenge and develop them. Inspire and motivate them. Communicate sincerely and often. Get to know them, let them get to know you,

3

and help them get to know each other. Listen to them. Hold them accountable. Offer feedback. Coach them. Counsel them when needed. Recognize and reward their good work. Ask them for feedback. Involve them in decision-making. Discover their strengths and dreams, and get them in the right positions. Get rid of those who can't or won't cut it, or who negatively impact others. And, perhaps most importantly, set a good example.

A team or organization is only as successful as the people who work there. A project is only as successful as those assigned to it. And an event is only as successful as those running it. In fact, the smaller the operation, the greater the impact made by each individual person involved. So, don't ever take for granted yourself or those in your charge. Instead, take care of both. And be enthusiastic about it! What's your most valuable resource? All together now … PEOPLE!!

The Challenge: Doing More with Less

A former boss of mine, Schwan's Consumer Brands President Mark Dalrymple, used to predictably conclude discussions about resource needs by saying, "Do you think it's Christmas? There's no Santa Claus in business." It didn't take long to get the point: we were not going to get the resources we thought we needed. "Yes, Mark, we understand. There's no crying in baseball, and there's no Santa Claus in business. Fair enough."

Another more common business axiom that has stuck with me is: "Profit is everything, and everything is profit." Translation: we need to keep our costs down, which means we, as leaders, will routinely be asked to "do more with less."

Profit v. Sales

It seems elementary that businesses would want to keep costs down to maximize profits. But, believe it or not, when businesses are doing particularly well, they don't always pay close attention to costs. Their time, in terms of profitability, may be better-spent growing sales than managing costs. For example, in a growing business, it may be better to spend 100 hours producing new sales that generate $10,000 in profit than it is to spend those 100 hours reducing costs by $2,000, especially knowing that as you cut costs, it gets harder and harder to find additional ways to save. However, in a business that is struggling to grow, it may be essential to cut costs, just simply to maintain a profit. In such a business, if 100 hours will produce new sales generating only $1,500 in profit, it may be better to spend those 100 hours cutting costs by $2,000. It's in those businesses, especially, that you hear mantras such as "Profit is everything!" Again, it's often a euphemism for: "We really need to manage our costs so we can remain profitable." The truth is that "profit is everything" in all businesses. But in growing businesses, you may be more likely to hear, "Sales are king" because that emphasis, in the end, produces more profit.

The best businesses, of course, focus on both growing sales and containing costs. So do the best leaders. So, I encourage you to manage your resources with one eye toward driving additional business and the other toward minimizing costs. However, in today's world of downsizing, re-engineering and "profits," be prepared, as I said, to "do more with less." Be prepared to get creative – by cross-training employees, forming external partnerships, leveraging new technology, etc.

Resource Planning

I think of resource planning in two ways. First, as a leader, you need to resource your plans. Second, you need to plan for your resources.

Resourcing Your Plans

Once you have developed a plan to achieve your desired results (see Chapter 1-Results), it's time to assign people, establish deadlines, and allocate money, facilities and equipment. This is known as resourcing the plan, and it's important in every leadership situation.

Tough decisions are often required when deploying resources, particularly when the resources available do not match those needed. It is important to communicate to people you lead about these difficult choices, your decisions, and the general importance of using resources effectively and efficiently. The more they understand, the sooner they'll be willing to work the plan at full tilt.

Planning Your Resources

It's also important to plan ahead for your future resource needs and ambitions. Even if you don't have a pressing need today for better facilities, equipment, talent, or budgets, you ought to be thinking about what you'll need a year from now, five years from now, or even 10 years from now. Think about the team, event, or organization you are ultimately trying to build – your vision. To get there, will you need an upgrade or expansion of talent? New or different facilities, locations and equipment? Additional funding?

It's never too early to take the first step(s). For example, if you eventually need to transform your staff so that it is more diverse, educated, credentialed, skilled, experienced, and geographically dispersed – as I once did – start planning now. You cannot transform a staff overnight. Communicate with your boss about the plan if it is appropriate, which it usually is. Communicate with your organization's recruiter, if is appropriate, which it usually is. Evaluate the likelihood of existing staff to quit, get promoted, transfer, or get fired. Along with your recruiter, begin networking – even if informally - for recruits whose qualifications fit the vision of your future staff. As existing people attrite, start building your vision one hire at a time.

Another example that comes to mind involves facilities. And, if you're a golf fan, you may be aware of this story. It begins and ends with a man named Mike Holder, who, at the time of this publishing, was the athletic director at Oklahoma State University and had previously spent 32 years as OSU's men's golf coach. Not long after taking over the golf

Oklahoma State University Golf Course

team in 1973, Holder made up his mind that he was going to make OSU the nation's best and most successful golf program. One of his ideas involved building a new golf course specifically for the college – one that would be plush enough to woo the best talent and challenging enough to make them better. As an idea, it was pretty "out-there." Colleges didn't have their own golf courses back then. Most still don't today. But Holder's vision was to be the best program in college golf, and he was bound and determined to make the new course a reality. Well, 20 years later, in 1994, after multiple setbacks that almost

3

killed the project, Karsten Creek opened in Stillwater, Okla., as the home of the Cowboy golf team. Holder personally led fund-raising efforts year after year, never giving up and finally securing the big donation that sealed the deal. All the while, Holder also was building up the program in other ways and using the golf course project as a symbol of OSU's commitment to being the best. It worked. In his 32 years, OSU won 25 Big Eight titles and eight national championships, produced 110 all-Americans, and placed first or second in 62 percent of its events. He indeed built what many regard as the nation's top men's golf program. And today, Karsten Creek remains one of Golf Digest's top rated U.S. courses and the #1 college course.

One more example of moving your resources from zero to something – perhaps my favorite example – involves my employers Frank Qiu and Ting Xu, owners of Evergreen Enterprises. They both emigrated from China to the United States to attend college as young people. They married soon after, with Ting becoming a computer programmer and Frank an insurance agent. Then one day, they stumbled upon an idea. While attending the Virginia State Fair, Ting noticed many flags and thought to herself that she could make better ones. Soon, the couple began to make and sell flags out of their garage, launching what has now become a $250 million business. I am routinely inspired by their truly American success story, and I think it offers a lot of valuable lessons about resources.

In terms of "people," they moved here not knowing a soul and not knowing the language. In the early days, they even enlisted the help of their parents, who kept up with demand by building flags in the garage while Frank and Ting worked at their "day jobs." Today, they have built an organization with more than 2,000 employees in three countries. In terms of "time," as I mentioned, they built the seeds of their company while working other jobs, with limited available time. They marshaled the help of not only their parents but other family members and friends as well. In terms of "equipment" and "facilities," they went from a single sewing machine and garage to automated machinery and facilities in both China and the United States. In terms of "money," they funded the business initially with income from their day jobs, but they also funded their educa-

Ting & Frank

tion by working in a Chinese restaurant. In addition, they always were frugal with the money they had, choosing to invest in their business rather than spend on themselves.

It is truly an incredible story of the American Dream. Like other entrepreneurs, the resource that meant the most to them was their idea. As Starbucks did with coffee, Subway did with sandwiches, and others did with bottled water, Frank and Ting saw opportunity in an idea so simple it may have seemed silly to others. Most critically, they seized the opportunity, becoming the No. 1 decorative flag-makers in the country and launching into a number of other product lines that help drive their business today. Beyond the idea, and their masterful use of people, time, equipment, facilities and money, Frank and Ting used their leadership qualities as resources. In fact, it was those qualities – intelligence, drive, risk-taking, etc. – that allowed them to build the other resources they needed to move from zero to something great!

3

There are many other examples of successful leaders planning ahead for resource needs or making something out of nothing. But I'm sure you get the point. Start thinking ahead, and take your first step now. Don't worry if it's a small step. You're at ground zero, and you know the deal – it's time to move from zero to something. You have a vision to achieve!

Reflections

Resources include all those people and things that can help you get the job done. And resource management may be one of your toughest, most important jobs as a leader. Not only do you have to use resources effectively, but you also have to use them efficiently, especially when they are limited, as they often are.

Think about the resources currently available to you, in terms of time, facilities, equipment, people and money. How could you utilize them more effectively and efficiently? How could you supplement them with support and assistance from elsewhere inside or outside the organization? Don't be afraid to ask your co-workers for input. A thorough understanding of the available assets may be the difference between being successful and not making it.

And don't forget to think ahead. Start planning today for the resources you want or need tomorrow. Go from zero – your current resources – to something else in the direction of your vision. Then reset the mental dial to zero and take another step.

Here are some additional questions upon which to reflect:

1) Do you know what resources are available to you internally and externally? (e.g. Information Services, Research and Development, Human Resources, Finance, Legal, and external consultants, etc.)

3

2) Have you thoroughly assessed your resource needs in terms of Time, Equipment, Facilities, People and Money?

3) In what ways do you demonstrate that people are your most valuable resource?

4) Do you secure resources following the appropriate rules?

5) Do you understand how others' roles can support your resource needs?

6) Do you build healthy and supportive relationships so you and your team can acquire the resources necessary to fulfill your work responsibilities and expected results?

7) During or after projects, do you reflect on how the resources you secured could have been used more effectively?

8) Do you make sure that you can realistically accomplish what you need to accomplish with the resources you have?

9) What is the focus at your organization, in terms of profit vs. sales?

10) What is the gap between your current and future resource needs? How can you begin to close that gap?

3

4

Rules

Rules: *Authoritative principles or regulations governing conduct, actions, procedures, arrangements, etc.*

I learned how to follow rules from my Dad. No, not the hard way. He actually made it easy to learn!

As a career military man, Dad lived and worked according to a strict code of structure and discipline. Naturally, this was reflected in our household; we had rules for everything. We had the standards: clean our plates at dinner, go to bed on time, always say 'thank you,' do our chores, and always remove our shoes indoors. But we also had to turn off the lights whenever we left a room, replenish the toilet paper whenever it ran out, and wipe down the shower and spout after every use. Even more unique: we had to wake at 6 a.m. every Saturday and Sunday for Dad's "golden mellow pancakes." More unique still: we had to go square dancing with Mom and Dad on every vacation.

Of course, I didn't always like Dad's rules. But I sure got good at following them, and, eventually, I grew to understand and appreciate their value. In retrospect, I always knew where I stood with my parents. The rules provided notice of their expectations. Rarely, if ever, was I confused or surprised.

By making the rules clear – announcing them, so to speak – my parents also bound themselves to applying them fairly. The same rules applied to me as applied to my brother and sister. Because Dad wasn't making up the rules as he went along, the rules also were consistent with each other. All of this helped reduce frustrations among us kids. Sure, we got frustrated, but mainly for getting caught! Or, for just being stupid! Not the hard way. The hard way to learn is by breaking rules you don't even know exist.

Dad's rules also served a teaching/learning purpose. Collectively, his rules were intended to instill discipline, keep me out of trouble, and condition me to doing the "right" thing. But, individually, each had a purpose all its own. For example, when my sister complained about doing the dishes and my brother and I teased her about it, Dad changed the rules and made dishes the job of my brother and me. He wanted us to experience her situation. The lesson? Empathy. Another example involved high school class rings. When I graduated, Dad told me that if I wanted a class ring, I would need to work and pay for it myself. Getting a job, which I did at 14, was one of Dad's big rules. The lesson? Work hard. Earn your own way. Become responsible. Naturally, I did not buy a ring. Hey, I was 18 and still learning!

A couple years later, when my family's income had improved, Dad decided to buy class rings for my brother and sister. About that same time, while I was stationed as a soldier at Fort Bragg,

N.C., I received a package. In it was a 1977 class ring. The lesson: fairness. That was the same lesson he taught when coaching my baseball team. I was sure I had earned preferential treatment by following his rules all my life, but of course, the preferential treatment never came.

I didn't realize it at the time, but Dad's rules were intended to benefit me, not him. That's why he also made sure I didn't get so caught up with staying inside the box that I couldn't think outside of it. He encouraged me to question rules and, on occasion, to consider ways of flexing, or getting around them, so

> **"I didn't realize it at the time, but Dad's rules were intended to benefit me...."**

long as the reason served a higher purpose than the rule itself. For example, we could break curfew but only to do nice things for others, like mowing the neighbor's lawn or giving Mom a massage. We also could tell white lies if it would prevent us from hurting others' feelings, like when commenting on food we didn't enjoy at a friend's house.

My ability to follow rules, work within them, and occasionally work around them, served me well once I entered the military. That background also proved valuable when it came *my* time to establish, communicate and enforce rules – both as a father and a military officer. It was even more valuable when I entered the business world, where rules can be less prevalent, less defined and more loosely enforced – in other words, where there is often much room for improvement.

4

Written v. Unwritten Rules

As a leader of yourself or others, your first rules-related task is to make sure you are aware of all the rules you must follow and within which you must work. In identifying all of the applicable rules, it is important to remember that some rules are written and some are unwritten. For example, in a business environment, you definitely will run across written company policies. Your business also will be subject to many written laws. At the same time, you may run across standard operating procedures, which may be written or unwritten. You also may encounter unwritten cultural norms, standards of etiquette, or "ways of doing things," i.e. conventional wisdom.

Rules	
Written	**UnWritten**
Policies	Norms
Laws	Conventional Wisdom
Regulation	Culture
	Regulation

Don't Play Blind

Keep in mind that you will find rules at many different levels – company policies, department policies, office or team policies, federal laws and regulations, state laws, city laws, company norms, office or team norms (aka House Rules), etc. Do your best to be aware of all such rules, and in some cases beware. To play the game otherwise is to play blind.

Think, too, about how rules apply to personal leadership and endeavors. Consider again the example goal of completing an Ironman triathlon. All such races have written rules regarding bike helmets, wetsuits, headphones, bike drafting, race numbers, etc. But someone pursuing such a goal also needs to be aware of many "unwritten rules" of training, regarding such topics as nutrition, stretching, hydration, recovery time, intensity variance, etc. To train without knowledge of such rules is to train blind, and to put yourself at a disadvantage.

This all may seem self-evident, but here are the challenges:

1) Others won't always go out of their way to share the rules with you, particularly the unwritten ones. In many cases, you must proactively seek them out or risk learning the hard way – by unwittingly breaking them.

2) In many organizations, particularly young ones, rules are not well defined. There may be too few written rules on the books, leaving unwritten rules to dominate. The rules may be inconsistent or applied inconsistently. In some cases, the rules may be outdated due to neglect over time. Or, there may be an utter absence of rules, leaving only "mob" rule. Leaders of such organizations may be unsure of the rules themselves, reacting fluidly to situations only as they arise.

Constructive v. Destructive Rules

I believe it is our duty to identify all types of rules, to support the constructive ones, and to work on avoiding or changing the destructive ones – those that inhibit success in one way or another. I do not advocate breaking such rules outright, but in certain cases, I would advocate working around them while simultaneously trying to change or remove them.

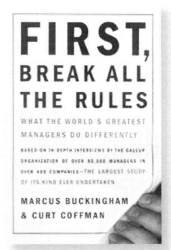

In his book, *"First, Break All the Rules,"* Marcus Buckingham asserts that great managers routinely break rules by tak-

4

ing the conventional wisdom about human nature and managing people, and turning it upside down. For example, he advocates rejecting the conventional wisdom, or rule, that people can be fixed. Managers should focus on the strengths of their employees, not the weaknesses, and instead should manage around weaknesses, Buckingham argues. Whether you believe this notion or not, it is a good example of addressing a rule that is often unwritten in the sense that annual appraisal documents usually ask managers to identify areas for improvement. The conventional wisdom is that those areas ought to be weaknesses, not strengths. If you buy Buckingham's premise, you as a leader may want to work on changing or avoiding that unwritten rule.

For example, you could speak with HR about your concept and see if HR would be willing to clarify in the performance management policy that "areas of improvement" do not need to be weaknesses. If HR leaders agree with you, they may even train other managers on your "strengths" approach. You also could ask your own boss if it's OK to focus on strengths instead of weaknesses. Or, you could build consensus among your peers. Or, you could simply not mention anything and go ahead with that approach yourself; after all, it is unlikely that the appraisal form specifically asks for "weaknesses." The gentler, more euphemistic "areas for improvement" is more likely, so you might not technically be violating any written rule, even if you are bucking the unwritten rule. Your example could lead to others noticing and eventually following suit. Sometimes, leading change in this subtle manner is most effective because it doesn't involve open advocacy, which can turn off the great majority who are not receptive to change.

In the end, you can go about changing or constructively working around a rule in any number of ways. The important thing is that you are aware of the rules and able to make smart decisions that advance your goals and those of the organization, while simultaneously keeping you out of trouble.

Action-Reaction-Counteraction (ARC)

A lot is made of office politics. The term has come to describe opportunistic, manipulative or devious ways of dealing with others. However, I believe its pejorative connotations are overblown. Certainly, I do not advocate hurting or damaging the fortunes of others in pursuit of one's own goals. That is what gives office politics a bad name. However, I do believe strongly in thinking ahead and considering how others will respond to your words and actions before turning them loose. I believe that is a healthy form of "playing office politics" – as healthy as thinking two or three moves ahead in a game of chess.

The model I use is a simple one I learned in the military – Action, Reaction, Counteraction – or ARC. For every action I consider, I also try to consider what the reaction will be, and what the counteraction (the reaction to the reaction) will be. Such considerations often influence what action I take, the way in which I take it, and/or the timing of it – and ultimately help ensure that my action achieves or accomplishes what I intend.

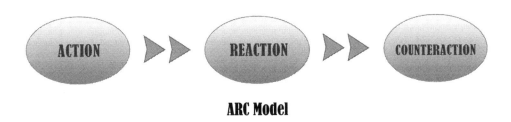

ARC Model

The ARC Model is potentially valuable in all aspects of life. But it's especially useful when dealing with rules – not so much when you're simply following them – but very much so when you're working to avoid, change or remove them. To illustrate, let's consider a fairly common scenario from the world of work.

As a leader, you will no doubt spend many hours training and mentoring employees. You will invest a lot. If you have hired well, those efforts will more than likely produce a valuable return, in the form of high-performing employees. Occasionally, though, you will invest in people who do not end up having the work ethic required for success. Still other times, you will invest in people who, despite your efforts, and despite theirs, just aren't up to the job, or whose best is only average. It will be frustrating. No one hires, hoping for an average employee. It also will be challenging. What do you do with employees who give you their absolute best effort but still falls short of expectations? Perhaps an employee shows up on time, works extra when needed, gets along with colleagues and customers, and presents none of the typical management challenges – but just doesn't have the skill or personality to produce the kind of results you really need. What do you do? Well, in most organizations, you will have a performance management process to follow. Those are your rules.

On a black and white page, and in the "rules," this question may be simple. You are probably thinking: If someone's performance is not up to snuff, regardless of effort, the performance management rules should eventually lead that employee to a different job or out of the organization entirely. That may be true. But few of us are blind to the colors of real life. We care about people. We value effort and hard work. And, let's be honest, we like people who respect our leadership. We also realize that a reliable, average employee, or even a slightly below average employee – one who is competent enough that we can focus on other issues – may be more valuable than the risk and cost of hiring and training someone new. All of these thoughts will weigh on you as you consider the ultimate question of whether to let this employee go, find him another job, or break the "rules" and give him extra time to develop.

I am not advocating a particular course of action. But if you are faced with this sort of scenario, I do advocate considering the reaction(s) and counteraction(s) to whatever action you are inclined to take.

For example:

Possible Action #1: Follow the performance management process to a 'T' and help the employee move on or out.

SOME POTENTIAL REACTIONS:	SOME POTENTIAL COUNTERACTIONS:
Human Resources (HR) may applaud you.	You may be able to use HR's good graces to maneuver around even more dicey situations in the future, when you really need HR's help.
Your boss may applaud you.	You may be able to leverage the good graces of your boss in acquiring outside help during the employee transition period.
Your boss may deride you if the team's overall performance dips in the short term.	You may be forced to work extra, justify the dip, and/or do more in the future to overcome the negative perception.

Possible Action #1: Continued...

SOME POTENTIAL REACTIONS:	SOME POTENTIAL COUNTERACTIONS:
Other higher-performing employees may applaud you for maintaining high standards.	You may be able to leverage the good graces of your top performers to cover for the employee's work.
Some employees may be disappointed to see him go because they simply liked him.	You may need to communicate more with upset employees so they understand your rationale. You may need to compensate the employees for their extra work. Or, you may need to prepare for the potential of losing another employee.
You will need to find, hire and train a replacement and possibly cover for the absence yourself.	You may need to enlist others to cover your other responsibilities while you work to fill the position.
Team performance may indeed decline initially.	You may need to communicate revised expectations to your boss and others, or you may need to adjust plans for later in the year so you can make up ground then.
Team performance may improve if those covering the work are more capable.	You may need to consider rewarding and/or otherwise recognizing those who go above and beyond.
Customers may react positively or negatively, depending on their relationships with the employee.	You may need to contact upset customers to explain the situation, ease their anxieties and ensure continued quality service. Or, if customers are happy, you may need to start thinking about what to do with your bonus check!
The former employee may be relieved and seek to find more suitable work, or on the flip side, may no longer be able to pay bills and support his family.	You will need to live with your decision either way. So, make sure it's aligned with your values – both business and personal!

Possible Action #2: Break the "rules" and give the employee more time to develop.

SOME POTENTIAL REACTIONS:	SOME POTENTIAL COUNTERACTIONS:
HR may scold or discipline you, especially if they advised you to take a different action.	Your boss may hold you in ill regard or discipline you herself. Or, if you had consulted her on the decision, she may view you as bold and decisive, offering you supportive assurances and political insulation from HR.
HR may support your decision to "flex" the rules in this case, especially if you lobbied for the exception by consulting HR in advance.	Your boss and the organization may reward you long term for being a leader of people, not just a cookie-cutter manager of processes and rules. Or, your boss may view you as weak and unable to pull the string when needed.
The employee may respond to your extra investment in him by improving more, or at a faster rate.	You will have time and energy to focus on issues other than hiring and training someone new. HR and your boss may congratulate you and reward you with additional leeway in the future.
The employee may regress if he perceives your extra investment in him as an absence of consequences.	You may lose customers, the respect of other employees, and the trust of your boss and HR. In addition, you may be forced to consider the decision again, only at a later time.
You may maintain customers that otherwise might be lost during the transition to a new employee.	You will have fewer new customers to acquire to meet your organization's goals and therefore can focus on other issues.
Other higher-performing employees may disrespect you for not maintaining high standards.	You may need to communicate more with upset employees so they understand your rationale.

4

Possible Action #2: Continued...

SOME POTENTIAL REACTIONS:	SOME POTENTIAL COUNTERACTIONS:
Some employees may, over time, slack off, because they believe you won't get rid of them.	You may need to communicate more with upset employees so they understand your rationale. You also may be boxed into managing other employees' performance in a similar, consistent way.
Some employees may see your extra investment in this person as a signal that you believe in people and will do whatever you can to help them succeed.	Increased loyalty may result in increased retention and performance among the entire team.

In this hypothetical, there are many ways in which you might go about avoiding, removing or changing the rules. And there are an infinite number of potential reactions and counteractions, depending on the situation, the organization, and the people involved. For now, don't worry so much about what you would do in such a situation. It's impossible to analyze without the details of a real scenario. Instead, focus on how helpful it is to think a couple of steps ahead when making decisions or taking action. Keep in mind that everything you do as a leader will cause, at a minimum, some sort of reaction – positive, negative or non-impactful. If you anticipate the most important reactions and counteractions, you will make better decisions and take better actions, particularly when it comes to "flexing" the rules.

Effective Rule Making

It is one thing to identify rules applicable to you and your team or organization. It is another to work hard at following the constructive rules and avoiding or changing the destructive ones.

4

It is yet another thing to create your own rules. But that may very well be your role, whether you formally help to write policy for an organization or simply establish protocol for your workgroup. Either way, I recommend establishing the following four components of effective rules: purpose, consistency, communication, and fair application.

Purpose

Make sure every rule has a clear and specific purpose in support of goals. Don't make rules just to have them. Generally, the purpose will be this: To provide *notice* of your expectations or those of the organization, and by doing so, to alleviate confusion, frustration and anger among those you lead. If a proposed rule would be counterproductive to the achievement of goals or would do nothing to prevent confusion, frustration or anger, consider shelving it.

Consistency

Make sure every rule is consistent with every other. Few things reflect inept leadership more than inconsistency.

Communication

In the best organizations and on the best teams, rules are not only clearly defined, but also clearly understood. It is the leader's role to ensure understanding. That starts with communicating the rules – often and via different mediums. And it ends with testing – not necessarily with formal pass/fail tests, but at least with observational tests. Can the people you lead effectively explain the rules to others? If so, you can be confident they understand the rules. If not, you have more work to do – either in rewriting the rules, communicating more, or communicating better.

4

Fair Application

Apply the rules equally to all you lead. In other words, don't bend the rules for some but not others. A common trap is to show more lenience with top performers than lower performers; we tend to rationalize by saying top performers earn more lenience. But what that really says is: the rule itself isn't important. And it tends to cause additional confusion, frustration or anger, diminishing the credibility of both the rules and you as the leader.

Rules to Live and Work By

Sometimes, creating rules that reflect your own personal philosophy or approach can be helpful too. Even if they're not official or "on the books," such rules can still serve a valuable purpose. For example, Gen. Colin Powell, the former U.S. Secretary of State and Chairman of the Joint Chiefs of Staff, once published a list of personal rules that served both him and those he led.

1. "It ain't as bad as you think. It will look better in the morning.
2. "Get mad, then get over it.
3. "Avoid having your ego so close to your position that, when your position falls, your ego goes with it.
4. "It can be done!
5. "Be careful what you choose, you may get it.
6. "Don't let adverse facts stand in the way of a good decision.
7. "You can't make someone else's choices. You shouldn't let someone else make yours.
8. "Check small things.
9. "Share credit.
10. "Remain calm. Be kind.
11. "Have a vision. Be demanding.

12. "Don't take counsel of your fears or naysayers.
13. "Perpetual optimism is a force multiplier."

– Source: My American Journey, by Colin Powell Jan 1, 1996

Powell's rules guided his own leadership approach. But they also encouraged and enabled those in his charge to display similar attitudes and behaviors. Even if the rules weren't "hard" expectations – or official rules of the Army or State Department – they served a similar purpose. Consider Rule #2, by which Powell let his employees know that it was OK to get mad. He probably didn't require it. But he allowed it, so long as they moved past the anger quickly. Such clarity is helpful to employees. Those serving under Powell could be confident that if they modeled the same leadership traits he espoused, they would excel. They also would avoid confusion, frustration and anger. For these reasons, I strongly encourage you to think beyond mere "do" and "don't" policy rules and consider also sharing your own personal "rules to live and work by."

Reflections

Your first opportunity to move from zero to something, with regard to rules, is to identify the rule environment within which you and your team must work. Make sure everyone knows both the written and unwritten rules at all levels. To do otherwise is to play blind, putting yourself at a disadvantage – no different than starting a game of chess without knowing the rules of the game.

Once you have identified the rules, you can make smart decisions about which constructive rules to follow, and which destructive ones to avoid, change or remove. As you work around rules or advocate for change, do so with care. Anticipate the reaction and counteraction before taking any action, and know when it's best to simply play along. Try not to compromise your integrity, but at the same time, remember that, in many cases, you don't make the rules – the company or its senior managers do.

When you do get the opportunity to create or change rules, make them effective by focusing on Purpose, Consistency, Communication and Fair Application. If you don't get to create anything else, at least capture and share your own personal "rules to live and work by." The people you lead will appreciate the window into your philosophy and expectations.

Here are some questions to ask as you assess and reflect on your own rules environment:

1)   What is an example of a written rule at your organization?

2)   What is an example of an unwritten rule at your organization?

3)   What are the constructive rules (written and unwritten) that you and your team must follow?

4)   What are the destructive rules (written and unwritten) that you can avoid, change or remove?

5)   What new rules are needed and/or would be helpful?

6)   How do you go about clearly defining any specific rules that may be applicable to a particular project or initiative?

7)   In what ways do you revisit the rules and communicate them as needed to ensure that everyone understands and is able to follow them?

4

8)   Does everyone in your charge understand the rules enough to explain them to others?

9)   What more can you do to help employees understand?

10)   Do you address performance when your employees fail to follow the rules?

11)   Do you follow the rules yourself?

12)   What are your "rules to live and work by?"

13)   Does everyone on your team understand the written and/or unwritten rules associated with the Leadership SOPs? For example, do they know the rules regarding the level of **risk** the organization is willing to tolerate when a new idea is developed and implemented? Do they know the rules regarding how to **relate** with one another on certain projects, and in general? Do they understand the rules related to **recovering** from long or intense projects and maintaining work/life balance? Etc.

Roles: *Functions or positions that carry with them expected behavior.*

Responsibilities: *Duties, obligations and burdens (expected behavior) for which one is answerable, accountable and relied upon and which require good judgment and sound actions.*

"One of the greatest responsibilities of anyone serving in the role of leader is to clearly define and communicate roles and responsibilities."

Once again, that profound quote is my own. Eat your heart out, Yogi Berra!

It's true. Roles and responsibilities clarify scope. They allow you and those in your charge to individually answer this: On what should I focus my energy and efforts, and on what should I NOT focus? And when people focus on the right things, positive results result. Again, Yogi, I hope you're reading!

ROLES & RESPONSIBILITIES CLARIFY SCOPE LEADING TO FOCUS PRODUCING RESULTS

Bland Before Grand

Like a lot of leadership topics, this seems, on the surface, like nothing more than common sense – hardly worth the cost of buying and reading a book. You may be thinking: "Of course a leader should define and communicate roles and responsibilities."

Once again, however, I often find that the obvious is overlooked. Too many leaders strive for the grand but in doing so, fail at the bland. To use a baseball metaphor, we constantly swing for the fences and, despite succeeding from time to time, we strike out more, draw fewer walks, put the ball in play less often, and, ultimately, lose more games. A stronger, more bland but fundamental approach would be to focus on recognizing balls and strikes, taking pitches out of the zone, and making solid contact when you get a pitch inside the zone, putting more pressure on the pitcher and defense. The latter approach may yield fewer home runs but will definitely produce more consistent runs over the long haul. In a lot of cases, it may even produce MORE home runs, which naturally result from the combination of attracting more pitches in the strike zone and making solid contact.

Let me be clear. I believe strongly in striving for grand achievements. Generally, however, I do not believe it is possible to achieve the grand without first mastering the bland. So,

5

as leaders we must be careful not to overlook the fundamentals and must instead focus on mastering them.

Roles v. Responsibilities

I'm not sure this topic is all that obvious anyway. Just consider the basic question: What is the difference between a role and responsibility?

If I am vice president of sales (a role), am I responsible for sales (a responsibility)? If I am a mentor, am I responsible for mentoring someone? If I am a project manager, am I responsible for managing a project to successful completion? The answer, of course, is "of course." But to leave it at that – role and responsibility indistinguishable – is to oversimplify the topic and to diminish the potential of both terms. Instead, for the words to have meaning, more distinction must be drawn between role and responsibility.

In my mind, the distinction is this: a person's role describes his or her "general" function, while responsibilities describe the specific expectations of that function.

Roles = General   Responsibilities = Specific

To say the VP of Sales is responsible for sales is not only a no-brainer; it's also nothing more than a restatement of her role. Despite the word "responsible," it says nothing of her specific responsibilities. In fact, if the boss of that VP defined no more specific responsibilities, the VP would be left to invent her own responsibilities or to make assumptions about the boss's expectations. Unless that is intentional – as in the boss genuinely intends to give the VP free reign and a blank canvas – then it is a recipe for miscommunication and failure.

Multiple Roles

My first and most memorable experience with roles took place when I was in basic training for the Army. My role was "trainee," and I never forgot it because Drill Sergeant Lamar wouldn't let me; nor would he let anyone else. We weren't good enough to be called soldiers until we graduated from basic training, he said.

To this day, I can still hear Drill Sergeant Lamar telling us that our only responsibility as trainees was to graduate and be-come United States Army soldiers. But that, again, oversimplified the expectations and served merely as a restatement of our role. In reality, we were responsible for all sorts of more specific things – everything from how we made our beds to how we

Ranger School

addressed the sergeants to how we handled our weapons.

Just as significantly, some of us also had additional roles. I wasn't just a trainee, for example. Despite being one of the youngest members of my platoon, I was tapped to be one of our squad leaders. At that point, I had two roles – trainee and squad leader. Each role carried with it different or additional responsibilities. As squad leader, for example, I was responsible for getting my squad of 10 men ready for formation, making sure everyone's lockers were ready for inspection, and communicating various information, such as our training schedule, among many other things. Indeed, I was held responsible for everything that did or did not happen with my squad – morning, afternoon and night.

5

The nice thing about the Army was that our roles and responsibilities were clearly defined and communicated so that we understood them. Sure, we heard the rhetoric about our only responsibility being to graduate. But we knew better. As trainees, we were inundated with constant training – classes, manuals and charts – that delineated our specific responsibilities and helped us avoid extra pushups. And I learned my additional squad leader responsibilities via intense daily mentoring.

In retrospect, I took away a lot:
- It's possible to have multiple roles.
- Each role carries with it different responsibilities.
- It's important for leaders to communicate those responsibilities in detail, in different ways using different mediums, and repeatedly. Doing so helps to ensure understanding and to avoid both individual failure (aka pushups!) and team failure (aka more pushups!).

Prioritizing

In reality, we all have multiple roles – both personally and professionally. Leader. Mentor. Father. Husband. Son. Employee. Project Manager. Homeowner. Club member. Musician. Committee chair. Spokesperson. Etc. One person might even play all of those roles simultaneously. And each role carries with it different responsibilities – duties, obligations and burdens for which one is answerable, accountable and relied upon.

As a leader of ourselves, we must know and understand all of our roles and the responsibilities they entail. Why? So, we can fulfill the expectations that others have for us and that we have for ourselves, and also so we can prioritize. The daunting fact is that most of us have more roles and responsibilities than we can handle. As a result, we have to prioritize those roles

5

and responsibilities that are most important to our happiness and success and that allow us to maintain a healthy work/life balance.

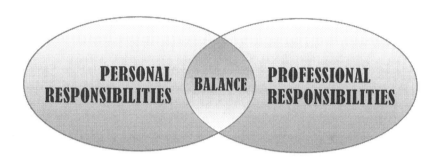

The FranklinCovey® company teaches people to identify their roles and then to identify their "big rocks" within each role. The big rocks represent the most important thing or things that need to be done in each role. It is a simple but powerful concept – one aimed at getting us to spend the bulk of our time on the most important things instead of being consumed by all the little day-to-day "rocks" that may seem urgent but aren't, in the scheme of things, all that important. FranklinCovey® effectively argues that we should fit the small rocks into our days around the big rocks, rather than the other way around, which can lead to neglect of the big rocks. For more information on this concept, I highly recommend FranklinCovey® and its time management products.

As a leader of others, we must help those in our charge understand their roles and specific responsibilities at work. By doing so, we help ensure that our team members prioritize appropriately and maintain a proper balance for themselves. That is good for the employee, but it's also good for the organization, which needs all employees focused on their most important responsibilities.

The DIFU Model: Difficulty-Importance-Frequency-Urgency

Whether prioritizing your own responsibilities or helping a team member, I suggest using a simple 1-2-3 approach, where 1 is the highest priority and 3 is the lowest priority. In determining priority, consider the *difficulty* of fulfilling the responsibility or task. Also consider its *importance* to individual, team and organizational performance and the *frequency* or *urgency* with which it must be addressed.

Priority 1. Responsibilities or tasks that are difficult and important and that absolutely, positively have to be fulfilled now and/or frequently. DIFFICULT, IMPORTANT, FREQUENT and/or URGENT

Priority 2. Responsibilities or tasks with varying degrees of difficulty that must be fulfilled but not necessarily right now or perhaps infrequently. VARYING DIFFICULTY, IMPORTANT, NOT FREQUENT and/or NOT URGENT

Priority 3. Responsibilities or tasks that would be nice to fulfill but only if time permits. NOT DIFFICULT, NOT IMPORTANT, NOT FREQUENT and NOT URGENT

This model is not scientific. It serves only as a guide. So don't get too caught up in which category you select for each responsibility. Consider difficulty, importance, frequency and urgency, and then trust your instinct on whether a particular responsibility warrants a 1, 2 or 3. It is usually easiest to identify the Priority 1 responsibilities, and that is where you and your team members ought to focus the most energy – both individually and as a unit.

5

Zero to Something
A Leader's Responsibilities

In the spirit of moving from zero to something, I recommend you start in the mirror by identifying all of the roles you play at work and away from work. Then identify and prioritize your responsibilities under each role.

To get you thinking, let's assume that one of your roles is "leader" of a team, department or entire organization. For which duties, obligations and burdens are you answerable, accountable and relied upon?

Obviously, this is something you ought to discuss with your own boss. For now, though, I'll share with you some of the responsibilities that I think most, if not all leaders, share. You may recognize them.

- Leaders are responsible for the bottom line – **results** – the sum total of all that happens and doesn't happen under their watch. They are responsible for setting and meeting goals and demonstrating success by effectively measuring the results.

- Leaders are responsible for strategic, forward thinking – for honestly and courageously assessing the current **reality** and clearly communicating a vivid picture, or vision, of the desired reality. They are also responsible for managing the change to the new reality.

- Leaders are responsible for managing **resources**, including people, equipment, facilities and budgets, among others. Getting the most from people may be a leader's single biggest responsibility.

- Leaders are responsible for identifying, establishing and communicating the **rules** within which all team members must operate.

- Leaders are responsible for clearly defining and communicating the **roles and responsibilities** of all team members.

- Leaders are responsible for fostering positive, **respectful relationships** among all team members. That starts with the leader earning his or her own respect by: demonstrating both organizational and technical knowl edge; leading by example; exuding both confidence and humility; listening effectively; accepting responsibility for decisions; demanding accountability from others for their decisions; and treating others with dignity and respect.

- Leaders are responsible for thinking "outside of the box" and taking calculated **risks**, based on prior analysis of risk and reward. They are responsible for not getting locked into "the way we've always done it."

- Leaders are responsible for demonstrating and demanding **relentless resolve** when it comes to the pursuit of goals. They are responsible for enduring and overcoming challenges.

- Leaders are responsible for creating a healthy work environment that promotes routine **recovery** activities to counter the stress related to a relentless work ethic.

- Leaders are responsible for **recognizing** and reinforcing the positive contributions of all team members. They also are responsible for recognizing subpar performance with coaching and counseling and for recognizing when others need training, advice or feedback of another sort.

- Leaders are responsible for constantly learning from their own actions and inactions and those of their teams, through the art of **reflective thinking**. They also are responsible for learning to think reflectively before making decisions by taking a step back to look at situations from other perspectives, including an outsider's perspective.

As you can see, this is a list of my R's - the SOPs of Leadership. If you are defining your own roles and responsibilities, as I recommend, go ahead and start here:

ROLE: Leader
RESPONSIBILITIES: The SOPs of Leadership

Be sure to review these with your boss. She is likely to have additional responsibilities for your list, as may you.

In addition, you or your boss may want to make the responsibilities more or less specific. The degree of specificity will vary, depending on the amount of latitude provided by the boss. For example, some bosses may choose to communicate a very general responsibility regarding results, such as: "You are responsible for meeting or exceeding the sales and profit plan." Such a boss may wish to provide you the latitude to achieve that result in whichever way you see fit. Another boss, however, may wish to prescribe more specific responsibilities that lay out the pathway or methods by which you are to achieve that ultimate result. Many factors go into such decisions. Rule of thumb: work together to make the responsibilities as specific as you feel is helpful. If they aren't specific enough, ask for more detail. If they're too specific, ask for more latitude. Just know that the higher you are in an organization, the more likely you are to be handed general, bottom-line responsibilities; at a certain point, you're expected to have the experience and expertise needed to determine the specifics on your own. On the other hand, if more specific expectations would be helpful, it rarely hurts to ask, or at least to confirm your assumptions.

Once you have identified your responsibilities in the role of leader, prioritize them using the DIFU model. And, then, don't forget to identify your other personal and professional roles and their related responsibilities. Stick with your four to seven most important roles. It is difficult to focus on more.

Establishing Others' Responsibilities

After you have clarified and prioritized your own roles and responsibilities, reset the dial to zero and start defining or refining the roles and responsibilities of those you lead. Work with them in doing so. And remember, the responsibilities should be as specific as the authority you are providing your respective team members and commensurate with their level of expertise and experience. For example, you could simply make an employee responsible for people management, which gives an experienced person the space to handle that responsibility in whatever manner she sees fit. Or, you could make her responsible for something more specific – such as maintaining 95-100% staffing, ensuring compliance with certain laws and regulations, training staff according to a specific curriculum, etc.

Generally, the higher up a person is, the less specific you need to be in defining responsibilities. On the other hand, for the typical individual contributor, specific responsibilities can be quite helpful, if not necessary. It is probably not enough, for example, to tell a veteran salesperson that you would like him to mentor newer salespeople. Sure, he has assumed the role of mentor. But, for what specifically is he responsible? Is he to mentor all new employees, or just particular ones? Is he accountable for their performance in any way? Is he responsible for mentoring outside of his normal work hours? Is he responsible for mentoring new employees according to any particular schedule or curriculum? I could go on and on.

We leaders tend to do a decent job at defining the responsibilities associated with our team members' primary roles. But my experience is that we are not so good when it comes to secondary roles. So, as you work with your team, don't forget to take a look at those roles as well. And remember to help your team members prioritize using the DIFU model.

Once you have established clear roles and responsibilities, you shouldn't have to do it over and over as you hire new people. I expect you will be hiring people to fill the same or similar roles and, if anything, will only need to tweak responsibilities to match the level of detail or specificity needed by a particular employee.

Communicating Roles & Responsibilities

Establishing clear, prioritized responsibilities is not enough. As a leader, you need to communicate frequently with team members regarding their responsibilities. You can do so in job descriptions, interviews, performance management discussions, day-to-day meetings, project plans, etc.

Job descriptions, in fact, are the perfect place to start. But don't stop there; unfortunately, job descriptions don't tend to surface much after a person is hired, and they also don't tend to get updated as often as roles and responsibilities change.

Your communication strategy should include helping team members understand both their own responsibilities and those of others, including yours. As I've mentioned before, we all tend to commit more energy when we understand how our roles and responsibilities relate and fit into the bigger picture of the organization as a whole.

Leading Responsibly

It is one thing to carry out one's responsibilities – one's duties, obligations and burdens. It is another to do so *responsibly* – exercising good judgment and sound actions. Yes, "responsible" is the root of both "responsibilities" and "responsibly," but the words are obviously not the same. So, since we have already discussed responsibilities, let's turn our attention to discussing what it means to lead responsibly.

My younger brother Glenn has taught me a lot about being a responsible adult and leader. I don't know anyone who has been so responsible from such a very young age. Upon graduating from a small town high school in North Dakota, he took off for the big time and headed to the demanding Air Force Academy in Colorado Springs, which seemed like a world away at the time. All of a sudden, he had to study harder than ever before. He had to work. He had to live within the disciplined culture of the academy. He had to get to know new people from all walks of life and from all over the country. And, before long, he had to support a family.

Today, Glenn is a successful business executive, the proud

father of two, a devoted husband, an accomplished amateur tri-athlete, a school board member and a community volunteer. He has roles and responsibilities to spare and yet manages to fulfill them all responsibly. While some of us end up focusing in some areas and sacrificing in others, my brother has managed to balance his commitments and take accountability for all aspects of his life. With the exception of my father, Glenn is the person I admire most. I'm the older brother; it was supposed to be the other way around. But it just goes to show that the qualities of responsibility know no age.

So, what does it mean to act and lead responsibly? In my mind, it means setting a good example by following

"So what does it mean to act and lead responsibly? "

the Golden Rule – treating others as you would like to be treated. It also means doing the right thing – all the time – even when no one is looking. In other words, passing the "red face test" – making sure your actions would not embarrass you, even if your mother were watching.

There are too many aspects of "living the Golden Rule" and "doing the right thing" to cover thoroughly in this book, and much of the topic is naturally subjective. Nevertheless, I will highlight a few of the key qualities of acting and leading responsibly, as embodied by my brother and other successful leaders I have been privileged to know.

5

Professionalism

The first of those key qualities is professionalism. Great leaders tend to look professional. They sound professional. They act professional. They exude it. But what does it mean?

Well, professionalism comes in many shapes, sizes and forms. It's the way you look – neatly groomed, neatly dressed. It's the way you communicate – clear, calm, considerate, positive, friendly, attentive, with proper language, etc. It's the way you carry yourself in front of a group or elsewhere – cool, collected, confident, prepared. It's the way in which you go about your work – punctual; reliable, disciplined; thoughtful; energetic; passionate; ambitious; innovative; a problem-solver; not a whiner, cynic or blame gamer. Do you look, communicate and behave like someone who can be trusted, who can work well with others, who can get the job done, and who can represent the organization in a positive light, according to general social mores? If so, then you are probably exuding professionalism.

Yes, it's true: image matters. But only you know whether your image reflects reality, so make sure it does, because another aspect of professionalism is genuineness. Be the real deal! Ultimately, most people will not judge you based on what you say; they will judge you based on what you demonstrate - on what you get accomplished or don't get accomplished. Do you model the behaviors you expect from your followers? And do your actions match your image and rhetoric? If so, then you are probably exuding professionalism.

Maturity

An aspect of professionalism that deserves its own heading is maturity. One of my previous CEOs felt so strongly about maturity that he identified it as one of a small handful of competencies essential to the success of top executives, in-

5

corporating it into our Senior Executive Development Program. This CEO wanted leaders who maintained their cool under stress and pressure. He wanted them to think clearly in those situations and not overreact. He wanted them to effectively maneuver through complex political situations. He wanted them to know when to encourage debate and/or move forward past debate. He also wanted them to be able to absorb criticism and sarcasm without losing control. In addition, he wanted his leaders to be respected within the organization and externally, and he felt that required them to display maturity at all times, even at social functions outside of the workplace.

Maturity sometimes gets a bad rap from people who associate it with being seriously boring or boringly serious. So, let me say this: playing, laughing and having fun are essential to a good work environment. And so is mature leadership. They are not mutually exclusive. It's OK for leaders to laugh, tell jokes, encourage games, and host fun events. It's possible to be mature at the same time. The mature leader doesn't stifle smiles and gag giggles, but, instead, encourages them. At the same time, the mature leader makes sure the fun and games remain appropriate and do not overtake or obscure the work at hand. Balance is the key.

Maturity – like many things – is hard to define precisely. In 1964, U.S. Supreme Court Justice Potter Stewart tried to explain "hard-core" pornography, or what is obscene, by saying, "I shall not today attempt further to define the kinds of material I understand to be embraced . . . [b]ut I know it when I see it." Maturity is similar in that regard. You know it when you see it. You also know immaturity when you see it. So, just remember, as a leader, all eyes are on you!

5

Integrity

Another attribute of those who lead responsibly is integrity. I grew up understanding that integrity means *doing what you say you're going to do* – in other words, walking the talk and demonstrating consistency of thought and action. Following and enforcing your own rules. I still think this is an important part of integrity, responsibility and leadership in general.

More commonly, integrity is thought to involve *adherence to moral and ethical principles* – a display of sound character. Honesty. Fairness. Consistency. Values. Zero tolerance for violence, harassment and prejudice. In my mind, these are obvious facets of integrity. I don't get particularly caught up in "values," since everyone has different value systems; one person may value family above all else, another may value health, and yet another may value career. But the basic principles of honesty, fairness, kindness and consistency are held almost universally, and they are essential to effective leadership.

More recently, I've also come to associate the word integrity with *accountability* and not shirking one's responsibilities. Leaders with integrity, in my view, choose to be accountable for everything they do or don't do and for everything their team does or doesn't do. They accept responsibility for bottom-line results. They do not create excuses or pass blame.

As you can see, the lines between professionalism, maturity and integrity often blur. And their distinctions are not all that important because, in many ways, one means the other and they all mean the same thing. To illustrate, consider these reflective questions regarding leadership communication:

Do you allow your team members to not only identify problems but to also provide solutions, or do you shut them off and not seek such input? Are you defensive when team members ask the question, "Why?" Do you encourage open communi-

5

cation, or does it end at your office entrance? Do you pass by people without acknowledging or responding to them? Do you interrupt team members when they are trying to help and, as a result, not hear them?

I would argue that these are questions of professionalism, maturity *and* integrity. Inconsiderate, non-attentive leaders who don't listen and are not confident enough to let others help aren't seen as professionals by their team or their peers, no matter how well they dress. They also are seen as immature – know-it-all teenagers with a title. Such leaders also are perceived to lack integrity because they do not treat others with respect and because their behavior often contradicts their lip service about "open door policies," "team efforts," and the like.

At the heart of all three qualities are two fundamental rules: Do what you know you should do (pass the 'red face test') and, of course, follow the Golden Rule: treat others as you would like to be treated. If you can stick to those principles, you are likely to lead responsibly.

Reflections

Remember that, by defining roles and responsibilities, you clarify the scope of expectations, enabling you and your team members to identify and focus on the top priorities so you can consistently produce results. It may be a bland exercise but it's fundamental to effective leadership and must be mastered before you can achieve anything grander.

Most of us have multiple roles at work and away from work, and each role carries with it different responsibilities. Think of roles as describing a person's general function(s) and responsibilities as describing the specific expectations within a particular role.

Beyond defining roles and responsibilities, leaders must

also communicate them repeatedly and in detail using various methods and mediums. It's also important to prioritize responsibilities; you can do so using the Difficulty, Importance, Frequency and Urgency (DIFU) model.

Start your efforts by identifying your own roles and responsibilities – focusing on the top four to seven roles; if one of your roles is leader, consider the SOPs of leadership as you identify related responsibilities. Next, start defining and/or refining the roles and responsibilities of those you lead, remembering not to overlook secondary roles. Make the responsibilities as specific as needed, based on the experience and expertise of your team members and the authority and latitude you are providing them.

In addition to your efforts regarding roles and responsibilities, make sure to always behave and lead responsibly – with maturity, professionalism and integrity; follow the Golden Rule and make sure you can always pass the "red face test."

Here are some questions to ask as you assess and reflect on your own roles and responsibilities as well as those of the people you lead:

1) What are your top four to seven roles – at work and away from work?

2) Which of your work roles is your primary function, and how does it fit in with other people's roles? Do you understand what others do well enough to help you lead your team or organization?

3) How clearly defined are your responsibilities within each role? Do you know what you are responsible for? Would it be helpful to define those responsibilities in more specific detail?

4) What method do you use to prioritize your responsibilities?

5

5) Considering your roles, when should you be a leader, and when should you be a follower?

6) How effectively do you delegate responsibilities?

7) In which roles do the people you lead serve? Did you help them identify those roles, including secondary roles?

8) Do the people in your charge understand how their primary role or function fits with other people's roles, including your own?

9) How clearly defined are the responsibilities within each of your team members' roles? Do they know what they are responsible for? Would it be helpful to define those responsibilities in more specific detail?

10) What method do you use to help your team members' prioritize their responsibilities?

11) What methods and mediums do you use to communicate to the people you lead regarding their roles and responsibilities?

12) How do you know whether the people you lead understand their roles and responsibilities?

13) How is it different to define roles for a cross-functional team vs. your regular work team?

14) How are roles captured in your organization? In writing (i.e. duty or job descriptions)? How are they reviewed, and how often?

15) Are the roles at all levels of your organization known? If not, what can you do as a leader to change that?

16) In what ways do you consistently behave and lead responsibly? At work? Away from work?

17) In what ways could you behave and lead more responsibly? At work? Away from work?

18) How do you go about demonstrating responsibility (or accountability) for your actions and results, whether positive or negative?

19) What examples do you set for the people you lead?

20) Have you ever failed the "red face test?"

21) How would you assess your adherence to the Golden Rule?

Respectful: *Characterized by politeness, deference and a high regard for the worth or value of a person, personal quality or personal ability.*

Relationship: *A logical or natural connection, association or involvement between two or more things or people.*

In the end, leadership, like life itself, is all about relationships.

One of the more important aspects of the human experience is that we are not alone. We all live in the presence of one another, and therefore, cannot help but experience life in the context of our relationships.

Leadership, similarly, implies a very specific relationship – that between leader and follower. And that's just the most obvious relationship. In fact, successful leadership depends on a number of healthy, productive relationships:

- **<u>Leader and follower(s)</u>** – *Our direct reports, those farther down the reporting chain and any others whom we may directly or indirectly influence.*

  These are often the most important relationships a leader must nourish. We achieve big things only by inspiring followers and working **"through"** them. (Some leaders may also see themselves as working "for" or "with" their followers, and both can be good philosophical approaches. But the most important concept to remember is that leaders are measured by what their teams achieve and, therefore, must seek success "through" their followers.)

- **<u>Leader and peers/partners</u>** – *Internal people who have similar or equal authority (peers) and external people or organizations with whom we work (partners).*

We achieve big things by working **"with"** these folks. (Good old-fashioned networking will help you develop more of these relationships. One of my former CEOs and mentors at The Schwan Food Company, M. Lenny Pippen, had an uncanny ability to build these relationships, creating a web of allies that helped him consistently mobilize support and resources both inside and outside the organization. To me, he was the ultimate relationship builder.)

- <u>Leader and customers</u> – *People we serve inside and out side of our organization, i.e. internal and external customers.* Ultimately, this is where the rubber hits the road. We must make sure we are always working, above all else, **"for"** our customers.

- <u>Leader and superiors</u> – *Our boss or bosses – perhaps our most important internal customer(s) and worthy of sepa rate mention.* The more we work **"for"** our bosses, the more support and latitude they will provide, allowing us to pursue and achieve even more.

- <u>Leader and organization/company</u> – *How comfortable, happy and aligned are we with our organization's values, vision, mission and goals?* It is important to have a good relationship with the organization itself because we work **"on behalf of"** it and achieve big things in its name.

- <u>Leader and own self </u>– *How comfortable and happy are we with ourselves spiritually (if relevant to us) and otherwise?* It's impossible to escape – we must live and work "**within**" our own skin. It is important for that inner relationship to be sound so as not to distract from our outward ambitions.

- <u>Leader and own family/friends</u> – *People to whom we relate primarily outside of the workplace.* For many of us, these are the relationships that matter most – the ones we carry through life, from job to job and cradle to grave. We work "**because of**" these people, laboring primarily to provide the resources that will allow us to enjoy these relationships to their fullest. When these relationships suffer, it tends to undercut and confuse our motivation for working in the first place, and so we must guard and protect these relationships always.

As you can see, leaders have a number of diverse relationships. And there is no avoiding them. These relationships are absolute. Whether you talk to your customers or not, you have a relationship with them. Whether you have met all of your followers or not, you have a relationship with them. Whether you have considered your spirituality or not, you have a relationship to it and with yourself. In all cases, there is a logical or natural connection or association. The question is whether that connection or association is healthy and productive, or neglected. But what does it mean for a relationship to be healthy and productive?

In my view, a healthy and productive relationship is one that is mutually beneficial and grounded in mutual respect.

Mutual Benefits

When a father loves a son, there is a mutual, or reciprocal, benefit. Each party enjoys both the giving and receiving of love. The son also benefits from the guidance, protection and teaching of his father, while the father enjoys the opportunity to once again see the world through the innocence of a child's eye. The father also benefits from the knowledge and appreciation that his genes will live on for at least one more generation. All of this, of course, assumes a healthy and productive relationship. If the benefits are stripped from either side, the relationship still exists but no longer remains healthy and productive. For example, if the father were to leave his son's life prematurely, the son would no longer benefit from Dad's guidance, protection and teaching; nor would the son be able to give or receive expressions of love. Even though the father can still rest assured that his genes live on, the relationship is one sided at best and no longer healthy and productive.

Personally, I do not believe the benefits need to be equal for the relationship to be healthy and productive. In fact, it is unreasonable to try to measure things that are so subjective. But I will say that the more equal the benefits are *perceived* to be, the more healthy and productive the relationship will be. The more people get, the more they are willing to give. And the more people give, the more they tend to get in return. What's important is to realize that, in any relationship, there is give and take. And the give and take must be reasonably balanced if both sides are to perceive a mutual benefit.

Think in terms of a simple boss-subordinate relationship. The boss theoretically gives a paycheck to the employee, who gives his time and talents. Sometimes, that basic measure of mutual benefit creates a healthy and productive enough relationship to achieve results. However, we all know that an employee who gives more (e.g. goes above and beyond, works overtime, provides leadership) tends to get more from the boss – more latitude, more opportunities, more pay, etc. And if he doesn't get more, he may no longer perceive the benefits as mutual, putting a strain on the relationship. At the same time, a boss who gives more (e.g. attention, mentoring, support) usually gets more from the employee – more leadership, more attention to detail, more effort, etc. And if she doesn't get more, she may no longer see the benefits as mutual.

As leaders, we must strive to nurture relationships in a mutually beneficial way, recognizing that the more benefit we provide, or give, the more benefit we can generally expect to receive. As benefits and mutuality rise, so too will the health and productivity of our relationships.

Mutual Respect

In addition to mutual benefits, healthy and productive relationships require mutual respect. To me, it's the most important ingredient – even more fundamental to a good relationship than mutual benefits.

Aretha Franklin

But what is R-E-S-P-E-C-T? It's obviously more than a classic, impossible-not-to-dance-to song by Aretha Franklin. We respect our elders. We pay our respects at funerals. We read about kids trying to earn respect on the street or playground. We might respect a parent. Or disrespect a colleague. We might even be able to sense a culture of respect when we walk into a leader's organization. But, again, what does respect look like, or sound like? As Aretha famously sang, we need to "find out what it means to me!" Better yet, how about I share my views, and then let you decide what it means to you?

In my mind, to respect people is to hold them in high regard for one or both of the following reasons:

- You **value** them.
- You **trust** them.

To be respectful, then, is to demonstrate that high regard by:

- Expressing appreciation – verbally or otherwise – for the value they bring to work, life and other people.
- Placing your trust in them.

When I think of people I respect, the name Dennis Jacobson comes to mind. He is a former boss who, when I knew him, never said a bad word about another person. He was always sincere and open to me and others, and he genuinely appreci-ated our ideas. He accepted us all as fellow human beings and earned our respect by being respectful. He was levelheaded. We could talk to him openly and never have to worry about being judged. I valued him in many ways. I trusted him with anything. And as far as I know, he felt the same way. We would have followed each other to the edge of the world, or at least far enough to see the edge.

The neat thing about respect is that it's always a two-way street, inherently characterized by mutuality, as it was with Dennis and me. Leaders need to both give and earn it. We must value others and at the same time be valuable. We must trust others and at the same time be trustworthy. It's simple, but not always easy. So, let's explore each of those concepts – value and trust – in a little more detail.

Value Others

The first key to valuing others is to actually **see the value or worth in every individual**. Everyone you deal with brings to the table diverse talents, personalities, work ethics, and ambitions. It's easy to see the value in the best and brightest of our fellow beings and natural to view all others in comparison. But it's more important – and indeed, virtuous, in my opinion – to see and cherish the unique value in everyone. It's there, – I promise. You just have to look. You might value talent in one person. A different talent in another person. Knowledge or skills in another. Experience in another. A different point of view in another. Ambition. Positive attitude. Work ethic. Emotional steadiness. Friendship. You name it. Everyone has something valuable to offer. As leaders, we just need to remove our blinders. In fact, we ought to seek out, embrace and encourage such diversity, as well as diversity of all types, because it tends to produce more ideas, more perspective and better results.

There will be those who challenge our ability to find value or worth. Even in such cases, it is NOT our duty to make them feel bad about who they are or who they are not. That would reflect insecurity in ourselves and would not win us any respect. Instead, I suggest starting from the proposition that every human life is worthwhile and deserving of dignity, at the very least. What is dignity? In this case, it is an appreciation for the gravity of the human condition. We're all equals in a sense – all looking to find or create meaning in an all-too-short life. And it's not easy. We struggle in different ways, but we all struggle. So, at a bare minimum, value the humanity in everyone, just as you value your own life.

Plato

OK, enough with the philosophy. Plato, I am not.

The second step in valuing others, after identifying people's unique, individual worth, is to **make sure they know they're**

valued. If we value people and they don't know it, they may assume we don't value them, and our relationships will suffer as a result. So, it's important to actually demonstrate that we appreciate others. We can do this in two ways: tell them or show them.

I recommend that you tell people you appreciate them as often as you can without going overboard and seeming less than genuine. Whatever you do, don't forget to tell them. The old adage that "you can get more with sugar than salt" is true, so spend more time being complimentary than critical. You can share appreciative comments at any time – in performance reviews, following a project completion, following a raise, after a major agreement, after a major

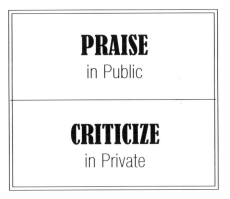

PRAISE
in Public

CRITICIZE
in Private

disagreement, at the end of a successful meeting, at the beginning of a meeting where everyone showed up on time, during a particularly tough day of work – whenever. The occasion doesn't have to be big or small. The person can be above or below you organizationally. You can appreciate people in private or public. In person. On the phone. Via e-mail. It doesn't matter. Just do it. Be genuine. And be specific about what you appreciate and value. You're not only showing respect that will likely be reciprocated, but you're giving the people you appreciate an incentive to do those same valuable things again.

In addition to *telling* people you value them, you can *show* them. For example, if you're a leader who places value on all human life, as we discussed earlier, you can show that by treating people with dignity. Be kind, courteous and compassionate, in deference to their equal standing as a human being. Once

6

again, it comes back to following the Golden Rule – treating others as you would like to be treated, or perhaps even better.

Showing others appreciation also can take the form of rewards and recognition, which we'll consider in more detail in a later chapter. Here, though, I'd like to focus on more subtle yet fundamental ways of demonstrating that you value people – by helping and letting them contribute, and by giving them your time and attention.

Let's start with the latter of those two because it's a simple concept: By giving people your time, energy and attention, you show that you believe they are *worthy* of it – that you value them enough to invest some of yourself. Make sure it's your best self, though – not a token or distracted piece, which can send the opposite message: that you don't value them.

Now, let's go back to "helping and letting others contribute" as a way of showing people you value them. Yes, we can show people we value them by, funny enough, actually valuing them. Sounds crazy, I know. But let me explain.

When someone asks for your opinion, how does it make you feel? When someone sincerely invites you to agree or disagree, how does it make you feel? When someone seeks out your ideas, how do you feel? When someone asks you for help, how do you feel? When someone listens to what you have to say and understands you, how does it make you feel? And when someone puts your thoughts, ideas and opinions into action, how does it make you feel?

I hope the answer to all those questions is that it makes you feel good and, more importantly, makes you feel valuable – because if someone wants your thoughts, ideas and opinions and makes use of them, you are in fact valuable to them. That, therefore, is the best way for a leader to show that he values you and the best way for you, as a leader, to show you value others.

All of this takes a certain level of confident humility. By spending more time in question mode than answer mode, by listening more and talking less, by asking for and being open to ideas or help, and by encouraging disagreement, you are admitting you may not have all the answers. At the same time, it shows you are secure and confident enough to sort out competing thoughts, make decisions, and share credit – all while helping others develop. When you can honestly say that others will freely tell you what you need to hear, versus what they think you want to hear, then you have hit the jackpot. At that point, you can be pretty sure they know that you value them.

Be Valuable

Of course, it's not enough to value others. That helps to show you respect them. But to establish a mutual, or reciprocal respect, you also need to earn respect by being valuable yourself.

That means you have to consider what others want or expect from you. In most work settings, they expect a professional – someone who is competent and positive, with sound character and a drive for excellence. They expect you to be committed to them and to the team, project, cause or organization; in most cases, they expect you to be even more committed than they are. They expect you to serve them by providing your support, time, energy and passion. They expect you to communicate and keep them informed. They expect you to listen to them and to fully utilize their skills, knowledge and expertise. They also expect you to be available and approachable.

In short, they expect a lot! And they have every right to, just as you have every right to expect a lot from the leaders you serve. But the more you deliver on these things, the more others will value and respect you. Don't forget – this is a book about more than doing a job. It's about leadership. It's about inspiring others to follow you. That requires a certain level of going above and beyond. Leaders cannot coast – not for long anyway. You can't hide behind your positional power. You need to create personal power, and you do so by creating value for not just your followers but all those with whom you have relationships.

So, be all those things you expect from and respect in your own leaders. Be worthy of emulation!

Trust Others

Now, let's consider the second half of the respect equation – trust. Valuing others and being valuable actually helps build trust by allowing both parties in a relationship to rely on the other to hold up their respective end of the bargain. But there is a lot more to trust. It's fragile. It's challenging. It can be strength-

"Trust?
Years to earn,
Seconds to **break.**"

ened over time. It can be destroyed in a heartbeat. And it can be difficult to regain.

One challenge for many leaders is trusting others. It seems simple enough. But leaders tend to come from the ranks of highly capable individual contributors. We were good at generating ideas and good at getting work done. That's why we got promoted. Once we're in the leadership role, however, our instincts often tell us that if we want something done right, we ought to just do it ourselves. But that can demonstrate a lack of trust in our followers, peers, partners, superiors, etc. Therefore, it's important that a leader learn to squash such instincts and consciously place trust in others. Don't wait for them to earn your trust. Instead, wait for them to break your trust. In other words, trust them until they prove untrustworthy. If you wait for people to somehow prove their trustworthiness, you are essentially treating them as untrustworthy without cause, which can destroy a relationship before it even gets started.

Trusting others means giving them responsibility. It means allowing them to make decisions, to make mistakes and to learn from them. It means challenging them to grow and achieve more and expressing confidence in their abilities. It means seeking their ideas and demonstrating faith in those ideas by utilizing or implementing them. It means confiding in others. It means freely sharing your own thoughts, rationale, influences and motivations, without fear that such disclosures will be leveraged against you or your leadership objectives. It means encouraging debate and disagreements without fear that doing so will breed unprofessional or damaging conflict.

Put another way, trusting others means not distrusting them.

Be Trustworthy

Probably even more important than your ability to trust others is your ability to demonstrate trustworthiness. If you trust others but can't be trusted yourself, people will lose respect much more quickly than if you are trustworthy but struggle to trust others.

Trustworthiness is also the most delicate area of respect.

6

Many different things go into it, and it can be destroyed by any one of them. I cannot possibly identify each and every aspect of trustworthiness. But I will highlight those that have surfaced the most in my career.

Number one, of course, is honesty. It's a deal breaker. As leaders, we have to be honest. It's what we expect from others. It's what they expect from us. It's an absolute requirement for any role model. If you lie, you will lose respect. If you become known as a liar, you will have no respect. Period.

Related to honesty is the topic of transparency, which gets us into the "degrees" of honesty. Can you cheat or beat the system without lying? Sure. Can you withhold pertinent information without lying? Sure. Can you manipulate people without lying? You bet. But in any such case, are you being dishonest? Probably. Good people can argue over specific situations. But most, including I, would argue that the more open and transparent you are, the better. You will be perceived as be-

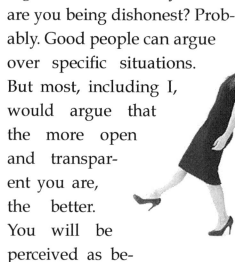

ing more honest and, in fact, will be more honest. But what does transparency mean? It means conducting yourself and your business in the light of day. Let people get to know the real you. Let people in on your decision-making process. Answer the question "why" whenever possible. Don't operate behind people's backs. Don't hide your warts or those of the business. Acknowledge your weaknesses and need for help. Don't sugar coat information. The more people see and know, the more they will trust. So, as much as possible, let others see and know all that you see and know.

Another key aspect of trustworthiness is fairness. Leaders need to be fair, just and unbiased. We need to embrace and encourage diversity. We need to treat others equally and apply rules equally, and if we don't, we need to have just reasons. Fairness also involves not taking advantage of people, even in benign ways. We must avoid unnecessarily or unreasonably intruding on or interfering with others' time, privacy and basic rights. If others see you as unfair in any way, they will lose trust and respect.

A third critical aspect of trustworthiness is fidelity. Keep your promises. Be loyal. Do what you say. For example, don't tell an employee you will nominate her for an award and then forget about it. If you can't or don't follow through on something, be forthcoming about it. People understand mistakes, so own up to it. If you cannot, they will find it difficult to trust you and will lose respect.

Finally, I would like to make the point that you can also engender trust simply by the general way in which you deal with others and approach your work. Start, as we've discussed earlier, by being professional at all times. People have a tough time trusting someone who is incompetent and negative or who has low standards or a shady character. Try also to, connect with people on a caring, personal level. Be someone others want to be around. Communicate "eye to eye and heart to heart." And, once again, don't hide behind your positional power; instead create and leverage a personal power derived from your individual strength as a leader. If you exude a professional and personal touch, you will gain more trust and more respect.

More on Respect

It is possible to respect people for only their value, only their trustworthiness, or only some elements of either. You might, for example, have very little appreciation for the tangible contributions of a boss or employee but still respect him greatly for being honest and sincere. It's also possible to not trust people who are politically manipulative but at the same time respect them for their ambition and accomplishments. Even within the value realm alone, it's possible, as another example, to respect the way a boss works with her team but not the way she works with her peers and her superiors. You might also respect people you don't like or agree with. Likewise, people may respect you in some ways but not others.

I would argue, however, that the more elements of trust and value that are mutually appreciated in a relationship, the greater the level of respect and the healthier and more productive the relationship will be overall. Think of the one or two people you respect most in this world. Do you value them? Do you trust them? Do you treat them fairly and avoid taking advantage of them? Do you give some of yourself to them? Are you kind and courteous to them? The answer to those and other, similar questions is probably yes. Sure, you respect people in different ways, for different reasons, and to varying degrees. But those who have earned your absolute full measure of respect – perhaps very few people, if any – most likely compel you by their own actions to value and trust them in every way, while you compel them to do the same. The point is that even if you enjoy respectful relationships, in most cases, there will be opportunities to improve upon and deepen the respect within those relationships. And I believe it is worth your time to do so, especially since respect can erode so quickly and take so long to re-build. Strengthen your respectful relationships now to avoid erosion.

6

Reflections

We have established that, as leaders, we engage in a variety of important relationships. We've also established that healthy and productive relationships require both mutual benefits and mutual respect. With regard to respect, we have explored how mutuality springs from both giving it (valuing others and trusting them) and earning it (being valuable and trustworthy). We also highlighted some of the specific ways we can establish shared value and trust.

But what can you do with all of that information?
Here is my suggestion:

1) Assess each of your own key relationships in the various categories – followers, peers/partners, customers, superiors, self, organization/company, family/friends.
   a. Target specific relationships that need improving and that you can influence positively.
   b. Decide what is lacking in each – mutual benefits and/or mutual respect.
   c. For each, put together a plan for improving the perceived benefits balance or the mutual value/trust proposition.
   d. Execute the plans – one relationship at a time if necessary.

2) Assess the relationships among and between the various other categories of people with whom you have relationships. For example, assess the relationships your followers have with each other and also assess the relationships your followers have with your customers. And so on.
   a. Look throughout your web of relationships, and target specific relationships that need improving and that you can influence positively.
   b. Decide what is lacking in each – mutual benefits and/or mutual respect.
   c. For each, put together a plan for improving the perceived benefits balance or the mutual value/trust proposition. Consider that you may

need to coach others on the elements of establishing healthy, productive relationships.

d. Execute the plans – one relationship at a time if necessary.

As you proceed, here too are some reflective questions to consider:

1) Who are three people you respect greatly? What is it that you value in them? What makes you trust them? How do you express appreciation for the value they bring to you? In what ways do you place your trust in them?

2) What characteristics do you share with the people you respect most? How are you different?

3) What more can you do to show people they are valued?

4) In what ways do you give your time, energy and attention to others with whom you have a relationship? How could you do more, or what could you do differently?

5) In what ways do you encourage and help others contribute? How could you do more?

6) In what ways are you valuable to others? What more could you do?

7) In what ways do you set a good example? In what ways would you like to set a better example?

8) In what ways do you demonstrate trust in others? What do you trust them with? Responsibility? Information? Insight into you? What could you do differently?

9) In what ways are you trustworthy? Are you honest, open and transparent with others? Are you fair? Do you keep promises?

10) Do you have a difficult time marshalling others to join you?

11) Do you communicate "eye to eye and heart to heart" or do you sometimes find yourself hiding behind positional power?

12) Do you talk behind people's backs?

13) Do you share your thoughts? Or do you keep people at a distance?

14) Are you perceived as someone who should be avoided or approached?

15) How do you deal with conflict?

16) Do you feel that people respect you? Why or why not?

17) How do you encourage others on your team to build healthy and supportive relationships? How do you show them?

7

Risk-Taking

Risk: *The possibility of suffering a harmful event or loss.*

The problem with risk-taking is that it sounds so darn risky. It sounds dangerous. Perilous. As if there may be dire consequences. It sounds like the realm of immature, naïve teen-agers. Like gambling. And we know what usually happens at casinos – you lose. Yes, to many of us, risk-taking sounds downright dumb!

Of course, rationally, we know risk-taking also can produce a payoff, sometimes a big one. We also know it represents a certain exercise of freedom – the freedom to make unconventional choices, for example. But for most of us – adrenaline junkies aside – the negative connotations are far more salient than the positive ones. As a result, risk makes us uncomfortable.

7

Comfort v. Danger

Nobody likes discomfort. Some tough guys might argue, but they'd be wrong. Even if you enjoy certain kinds of discomfort (fighting or endurance challenges, for example), the fact that you enjoy something means, by definition, that it actually brings you comfort. Whatever brings you comfort, it's human nature to seek it out and to live, as they say, in the "comfort zone." It's also human nature to avoid danger, whatever that looks like to you. More comfort. Less danger. That may as well be the human motto. The motto for all species perhaps.

Comfort Zone   ⟷   Danger Zone

Unfortunately, change tends to move us out of the comfort zone and toward the danger zone. Change is frightening, to one degree or another, because of the risk that we will not return to the comfort zone, that our discomfort with the change will persist. Change is difficult because natural forces constantly pull us back toward our comfort zone.

Then again, change cannot and should not be avoided. Certainly, as leaders, our responsibility is to actually create change. Not too many people are paid to maintain the status quo, unless of course that itself is a change. Our job, then, is to take risks, to manage them, and, ultimately, to establish new comfort zones for our employees, our customers, our business, and ourselves.

"I am always doing that which I cannot do, in order that I may learn how to do it." – Pablo Picasso

Take more risks. Create more change. Conquer the world, right? Well, maybe not the world. But it's true that if we want to do great or extraordinary things, we probably need to take more risks than our peers and competitors. The key, however, is to take more risks, not necessarily bigger risks.

Take More Smart Risks, Avoid the Dumb Ones

There is such a thing as a dumb risk. Shooting heroin, for example. Or, jumping off a cliff into unfamiliar water. Most of us are pretty good at avoiding these dumbest of risks. The problem is: in our attempt to avoid dumb risks, many of us develop too much caution. As a result, we end up avoiding the smart risks too. It is just part of how we're wired. But it's also an opportunity. If we can take more smart risks than the average person or average leader, we will earn the payoff of creating more change. We will establish new comfort zones. Generate progress. Experience success.

> *"Progress always involves risks. You can't steal second base and keep your foot on first." – footballer Frederick Wilcox*

Let me be clear. I do not advocate taking bigger risks, unless they are smart. And I don't advocate taking any dumb risks. I recommend taking more smart risks. The obvious question: What makes a risk smart?

Calculate the "Smartness"

My mom began teaching me about risk at a young age. I can still hear her as though she were sitting right in front of me. She always used to ask, "Arnold, are you sure you want to do that?" No matter the answer, her follow up was always the same: **"Why?"** By constantly prompting me to consider the rationale for my decisions before I made them, she trained me to ask: What happens if I do, and what happens if I don't? That, as it turns out, is the essence of calculating the "smartness" of risk.

7

The legal and insurance worlds take it a step further, calculating two specific factors into their what-if scenarios: likelihood and consequence. For example, flying in a commercial passenger airplane carries with it a 1 in 11 million chance (likelihood) of death (consequence). That is the basic calculation of risk, according to common risk management practices, which focus on the potential for downside. When it comes to making smart decisions, however, it is also necessary to calculate the upside in terms of likelihood and consequence. In this case, there is a 99.9999999 percent chance that you will not die and will save time, at the very least.

	Upside (likelihood and consequence)	**Downside** (likelihood and consequence)
What happens if I DO fly in a commercial airplane?	99.9999999% chance of saving time without dying; therefore, more time to spend at destination or elsewhere	00.0000001% chance of death

Now, we cannot forget to also consider: "What happens if I don't?" In this example, if you decide not to fly, you also are incurring a risk – the risk of missing out on other opportunities due to the extra time, and possibly money, you need to spend making the trip by car instead. You also incur the risk of dying in a car crash. If you abandon the trip altogether, you run the risk of any downsides associated with not achieving your original travel objective. If it was supposed to be a relaxing vacation, for example, you run the risk of developing more stress.

These are the calculations that go into determining whether a

	Upside *(likelihood and consequence)*	Downside *(likelihood and consequence)*
What happens if I DON'T fly in a commercial airplane?	100% chance of not dying in plane crash.	CAR ALTERNATIVE 100% chance of spending more time to reach destination; therefore, less time to spend at destination or elsewhere. Plus, a 1 in 2.4 million chance of dying in a car accident instead. NO TRIP ALTERNATIVE 100% chance of not accomplishing original objective unless by other means, which would have its own risks

risk is a smart one. Sometimes, these calculations can be quickly processed in the head. Other times, it helps to think through them in more detail and to write them down, especially in the early stages of trying to improve our risk-taking skills. Either way, here's the harder part: We still need to interpret the calculations and apply judgment in deciding whether to go for it. We cannot simply plug in the data and expect an answer to appear. The calculations will, however, make it *easier* for us to make a confident, informed, smart decision.

My example of whether to fly can be answered easily by most people who look at the calculations: book the flight! If you do it, the likelihood of the upside is extremely high, and the upside is meaningful, while the likelihood of the downside is infinitesimally low, albeit very severe. At the same time, the downside of not flying is pretty great and, in most respects, 100% likely.

Using my risk calculation table, let's look at a couple of other examples that demonstrate two extremes – the smartest of risks (asking a girl for a date) and the dumbest of risks (shooting heroin). There may be smarter and dumber risks, but these rank right up there in my mind.

THE SMARTEST OF RISKS – e.g. Asking for a Date		
	Upside	**Downside**
What happens if I DO?	HIGH LIKELIHOOD of UPSIDE – good chance she'll say yes unless you're a jerk or dirty, or she's taken BIG POSITIVE CONSEQUENCE – potentially love	LOW LIKELIHOOD of DOWNSIDE – If you're clean and polite, and she's not taken, it's relatively unlikely she'll say no SMALL NEGATIVE CONSEQUENCE EVEN IF DOWNSIDE HAPPENS – temporary blow to self esteem
What happens if I DON'T?	LOW LIKELIHOOD of UPSIDE – Have to rely on girls to ask you for a date SMALL POSITIVE CONSEQUENCE EVEN IF UPSIDE HAPPENS – you'll have to settle for whoever seeks you out, which could lead to something less than love	HIGH LIKELIHOOD OF DOWNSIDE – if you never ask, chances are pretty high you will never receive BIG NEGATIVE CONSEQUENCE – potentially, no love

THE DUMBEST OF RISKS – e.g. shooting heroin		
	Upside	**Downside**
What happens if I DO?	LOW LIKELIHOOD of UPSIDE – a rush of relief, or high, is likely but happiness is not SMALL POSITIVE CONSEQUENCE EVEN IF UPSIDE HAPPENS – any happiness will be fleeting	HIGH LIKELIHOOD of DOWNSIDE – effects always fade, and there's a chance for overdose and addiction BIG NEGATIVE CONSEQUENCE – heroin kills and costs money
What happens if I DON'T?	HIGH LIKELIHOOD of UPSIDE – health, more money in pocket BIG POSITIVE CONSEQUENCE – longer, happier life	LOW LIKELIHOOD OF DOWNSIDE – small chance of anxiety at parties perhaps SMALL NEGATIVE CONSEQUENCE EVEN IF DOWNSIDE HAPPENS – such anxiety is fleeting

7

When I was younger, I actually took fewer risks because of the caution my mom instilled. I became good at thinking twice. I almost always considered "What if I do" and "What if I don't," but under her watchful eye, the safer route usually seemed best. I wasn't mature or skilled enough to seriously calculate the likelihood and magnitude of potential consequences; nor did I have the judgment to make savvy decisions based on those calculations. I also may have assumed that when she asked "why," it was her way of saying "don't." What can I tell you? I was just a boy!

As I grew older, however, and learned to calculate my risk-taking options more appropriately, I intentionally took more and more risks. To this day, my mom seems to shake her head a lot. I guess when it comes to me, she's still pretty risk averse. Perhaps that is the motherly way. But mom, if you're reading this, I hope you can see that I do not take risks lightly, thanks in large part to you. I take them only after careful calculation. That doesn't mean my risk-taking always pans out. But over the long run, in sum total, it has led to much more positive change than I could have achieved otherwise.

Consider a couple of relatively recent risks I took. The first was to train for and compete in a 2007 Ironman triathlon competition, an endurance test comprised of a 2.4-mile swim, a 112-mile bike and then a 26.2-mile run. The other risk was writing this book.

In the first decision, regarding the Ironman, it really came

IRONMAN OR NO IRONMAN		
	Upside	**Downside**
What happens if I DO?	I would almost certainly improve my health and would very likely improve my discipline and time-management skills as well. There is no guarantee that I would make it to the finish line, but I have a good track record when it comes to matters of effort and stamina, so I would rate the likelihood as moderately high to high, and the sense of achievement here would be huge.	Training takes time, so it's very likely I would have less time to spend at work and home. On the other hand, I have been seeking more work-life balance, and my wife is very supportive of this idea, so it may not be such a bad consequence. Plus, once the event is over, I could return to a more normal schedule. Ironman training involves pain and a moderate likelihood of injury, though probably not severe. It also requires money for equipment, though I have the budget. In addition, there is a low to moderate chance that I would not make it to the finish line, which would be devastating after such a big personal investment.
What happens if I DON'T?	The upside of not doing an Ironman would be a 100% likelihood that I would have more time for work, family and other interests. It's also 100% likely I would not endure any of the pain of training. In other words, everything would remain as it is today, in terms of my time and health. That's not an enormously positive consequence in my eyes.	If I don't do an Ironman, it's 100% likely I will always wonder "what if." I suspect I will regret it – maybe not immediately, but eventually, especially when I am too old to have the option anymore. I have been doing shorter triathlons and have made the sport a part of my life. To stop short of the sport's ultimate test would leave me disappointed in myself.

down to this – was I willing to risk time, money, physical pain and possible failure for improved health and the satisfaction of achieving a big goal? The upside was significant in my view and quite likely if I just committed to it. The downside? Well, I made the decision that even if I failed, I could live with the lost time (and other opportunities) and money, as well as whatever pain I had to endure. I also decided I could live with failure itself. I

BOOK OR NO BOOK		
	Upside	**Downside**
What happens if I DO?	I've been leading and studying leadership my entire adult life. For the past decade or so, I've wanted to capture my thoughts on the subject in a book. It has been on my bucket list, and getting it done would, with 100% likelihood, provide me with a huge sense of satisfaction and achievement. As a goal-oriented person, that would be a significantly positive consequence. I also could earn book sales and related consulting income, though practically speaking, the likelihood is low to moderate. The magnitude of such a consequence, however, could range from low to high. Finally, even if the book is not a New York Times bestseller, it is something I definitely would be able to use in my day job as a Human Resources executive, and that would be moderately to highly valuable.	It's 100 percent likely I would need to spend time and money to write, edit and publish the book. I have the budget, but the investment would still be significant. From a pure monetary standpoint, I would even say there is only a low to moderate chance I would get a return on my investment. There also is a chance that no one would read the book or that those who do would not find it valuable. I have an ego like anyone else, so that could hurt, especially if my wife pans it! On the other hand, the book would be based on proven concepts. I'm also working with a trusted and competent collaborator. In addition, my main objective is to fulfill a personal goal, have a book I can use in my own work, and leave something meaningful behind for my family. Critical and/or commercial success would be nice but is not needed.
What happens if I DON'T?	The upside of not writing the book is that I would not be out any time or money. It's 100% certain I could focus on other responsibilities and interests. I also, with 100% certainty, would not open myself up to criticism. Both of these upsides represent the status quo, which for me, is not bad but not particularly positive. I prefer growth.	The downside of not writing the book would be lost opportunity and regret, both of which would be 100% likely. I hate not achieving goals or leaving items on my bucket list. I do not like to wonder "what if." It leaves me unfulfilled. At the same time, no one but me (and probably my wife) would care or notice if I didn't get this done.

would come away healthier either way. And if I did fail, I would live to try again or at least be able to move on without wondering "what if." This was not an easy decision, but it was easier because of careful calculation. In the end, I went for it and not only

7

completed the race, but finished in respectable time too. I was a proud Ironman. The risk paid off.

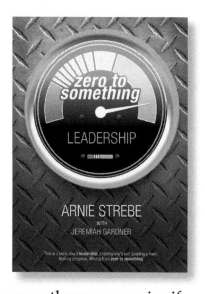

As for the second decision, regarding the book, you already know the end of that story. Again, the decision boiled down to whether I was willing to risk time, money and possible failure for the chance to fulfill a dream and possibly further my career. The difference between this and the Ironman decision was that, in this case, there was a significant chance of failure, at least from a critical and commercial standpoint. I began the book on spec, as they say, thinking to myself: just write it and see if anyone likes it. I knew it was unlikely that I would be able to do much more than publish a few hundred copies myself, use them at work, and distribute them to friends, family and colleagues. I also knew that people might not like the book or find it valuable in any way. That is not to say I didn't feel I had something valuable to share. I did, and I genuinely wanted, and still want, this book to really help people who lead or aspire to lead. I just knew the long odds of hitting the big time. After carefully calculating the risk, though, I decided it was worth the investment, even if no one outside my family and friends ever read or liked a word. The book would mean enough to me in my own job, and it would allow me to pass down a piece of myself to my children. I was willing to risk the rejection of others. It wasn't an easy decision, and as I write this, the jury is still out. So, please post your positive comments on *www.zerotosomething.com*. As for negative comments, please post your positive ones at *www.zerotosomething.com*!

7

"You'll always miss 100% of the shots you don't take."
– hockey great Wayne Gretzky

If you work in the business world, you will run into countless opportunities to take risks. Every decision, in fact, involves some level of risk. You may find yourself asking questions such as: Do I ask for a raise? Do I introduce a new process? Or a new product? Do I take a chance on hiring someone with less experience but more ideas? Do I ask tough questions about the boss's plan? Do I take on a new, challenging job or assignment, even if the circumstances are not ideal? Do I invest in new capital projects? Do I buy? Do I sell? Do I merge? Do I reorganize?

Elsewhere, you might face questions such as: Do I start my own business? Do I ask her to marry me? Should we have a baby? Is it the right time to buy a house? Can we afford a vacation?

Tough decisions are tough because they involve risk. Just remember: I don't recommend taking all risks all the time. But if you want to create change and forge progress, do make the smart ones. Calculate the likelihood and magnitude of the upside, as well as the downside – both in terms of "what if I do" and "what if I don't." Consult colleagues, employees, family members and/or others as needed. Then, apply your best judgment and make a decision. Can you live with the downside if it happens? Can you minimize the hazards? Have you tried this before and learned anything? Do you have a support system? Who else are you exposing to the risk, and have you calculated the upside and downside for them? Can you maintain control in the face of the expected discomfort? Is it the right time? How important is the upside to the happiness and success of you or others? Is the upside high or even limitless? Can you fully commit? So long as you carefully think through the calculations, in my view, you will avoid a dumb decision and make a smart one, regardless of the eventual outcome.

The Gut Check

I have mentioned it a couple of times already. But it bears repeating. No matter how much calculating we do, in the end, we have to make a judgment call. We have to follow our gut. The calculations merely serve the purpose of informing our gut so we are able to trust it. The more we prepare for a decision, the more we should be able to trust what our gut tells us. Likewise, the more decisions we make, the more trust we will develop in our risk-taking and decision-making instincts.

> *"You've got to learn your instrument. Then, you practice, practice, practice. And then, when you finally get up there on the bandstand, forget all that and just wail." – jazz musician Charlie Parker*

Fear Not, Fail Fast

Our risk-taking will not always produce the results we want. But that's no reason to fear failure. No one has a crystal ball. The most we can reasonably expect from ourselves is that we make the **best decision at the time**. So, do your calculations and trust your gut. Most times, an early decision leads to faster progress, even if it's wrong or requires a change later on. It's important to get the ball rolling.

> *"Trust your own instinct. Your mistakes might as well be your own, instead of someone else's."*
> *– filmmaker Billy Wilder*

At the same time, prepare for failure. Don't fear it. Setbacks will happen. But do sweat it. And sweat it ahead of time. Prepare to fail fast so you can learn and move on toward the goal. That means creating alternate or contingency plans.

It also means being prepared to admit when your decision is wrong so you can change course quickly. We cannot afford to hold fast to ill-fated decisions, especially out of pride. Successful risk-taking and strong leadership requires that we be open about our mistakes so we can change quickly.

If we are confident about the process and our ability to change quickly, we should be able to jump in and fully commit to our decisions early. Over-analyzing and taking longer to make decisions can slow down progress, even if it reduces mistakes. So, there is a balance to strike. We still need to calculate. But then we need to trust our gut, make the best decision at the time, and prepare to adjust quickly when needed. Be confident about that. Trust the process. Don't wait for the stars to align.

"A man would do nothing, if he waited until he could do it so well that no one would find fault with what he has done." – Cardinal Newman

Consider this too: if we're not making mistakes, we're probably not taking enough risk. We're probably not pushing the limits at all, and that's what produces growth. A snowboarder who doesn't fall, for example, is a snowboarder who is probably no longer improving. A triathlete who never experiences pain is a triathlete who is not getting faster. In that sense, mistakes and missteps are a good thing – part of acclimating to new territory. So, again, don't fear making the wrong decision. Embrace mistakes as an inevitable sign that you are indeed taking the risks needed to strengthen yourself, your team and your organization.

"Only those who will risk going too far can possibly find out how far it is possible to go." – author T.S. Eliot

The only thing we should fear is inaction. Doing nothing is not neutral. In most cases, it is negative because it precludes us from the chance of winning. And we can't win if we don't play. Taking risks, at the very least, gives us a chance to win.

<u>Lloyd:</u> *What do you think the chances are of a guy like you and a girl like me... ending up together?*
<u>Mary:</u> *Well, Lloyd, that's difficult to say. I mean, we don't really...*
<u>Lloyd:</u> *Hit me with it! Just give it to me straight! I came a long way just to see you, Mary. The least you can do is level with me. What are my chances?*
<u>Mary:</u> *Not good.*
<u>Lloyd:</u> *You mean, not good like one out of a hundred?*
<u>Mary:</u> *I'd say more like one out of a million.*
[pause]
<u>Lloyd:</u> *So you're telling me there's a chance... YEAH!*
– scene from the movie Dumb and Dumber

Next Steps

Obviously, it is easier to write or read about being fearless than it is to actually face the uncertainty that comes with taking risks. So, to begin improving our risk-taking, it is important to spend a little time thinking about what exactly prevents us from pulling the trigger on more risk-taking opportunities. Think about yourself for a moment. Is it fear of rejection? A need for approval? The need to always be right? Fear of hurting others? The need to avoid guilt? A lack of belief in yourself or others? A desire to avoid conflict? The need to understand every detail? Denial that change is needed or even possible?

7

A belief that it's not your problem? Are you more focused on your image and reputation than what you want to accomplish?

Do a little self-therapy. Once you understand your roadblocks to risk-taking, remind yourself what happens when you don't take risks. Problems go unresolved. Change doesn't happen. You become dependent on others. People eventually stop listening to your "yes, buts" and then stop helping. You start to feel stuck. Unhappiness sets in.

Next, think about a specific risk-taking opportunity with which you struggle. What is keeping you from solving a particular problem? What is uncertain, and how does that make you feel? What do you need to take the necessary risk(s)? What are you willing to sacrifice or invest to see your decision through? How will you deal with your own personal needs, i.e. for approval or perfection? What is the worst possible outcome, and in the grand scheme of things, is it all that bad?

When it comes to asking for a date or a raise, or deciding to train for an Ironman or write a book, the worst-case scenario is not too severe. Yet, many of us still tend to avoid such risks, mainly due to ego rather than the potential for any real loss. Even more of us avoid the more consequential risks, such as starting a new business, which, in the worst case, can lead to bankruptcy. But I have consulted with new entrepreneurs who explained to me that bankruptcy is not such a doomsday after all. We were born broke, they said. Most of us graduate from college broke. And most of us will survive going broke again. Heck, they reminded themselves, we die broke, too. From that perspective, the worst-case scenario was not as earth shattering as it may have seemed otherwise.

"Never be afraid to try something new. Remember, amateurs built the ark; professionals built the Titanic." – Author Unknown

In the interest of moving from **zero to something**, consider identifying a single risk-taking opportunity. Go through your calculations, listen to your gut, make the best decision at the time, prepare for the need to change course, and see what happens. You will either achieve the identified upside of your decision, or you will learn from the downside. Next, do it again. You will get more comfortable and confident with each risk you take. Remember, the goal is to take more smart risks than your peers and competitors. Pursue that goal one risk at a time. Zero to something.

Promote Risk-Taking

Part of risk-taking and leading is going first, rather than waiting for others to blaze the trail. Now, I'll admit that in some situations, it makes sense to intentionally aim for second – to be second to market with a new product, for example. It allows you to avoid the mistakes of whoever goes first. That is the safer route and might be the right strategy if you are not in a position to tolerate more risk. But it's more of a stay-alive strategy than a winning strategy.

"Destiny is not a matter of chance, it is a matter of choice; it is not a thing to be waited for, it is a thing to be achieved."
– William Jennings Bryan

The winning strategy is to be out front – to identify new, risk-taking opportunities before you read or hear about them elsewhere. As a leader, it behooves you to create a culture of innovation within your sphere of influence. My belief is that brilliance is hidden within many organizations. It lies hidden on the front line, within middle management and all points in between. People aren't even aware of it in many cases. They write off their own ideas as "nuts" or don't even bother to turn their knowledge and observations into ideas because no one is asking for ideas.

We need to live by Mark Twain's old saying, *"If you always do what you always did, you will always get what you always got."*

More importantly, we need our entire team or organization to live by that creed. We need to ask our followers big questions, seek ideas, discourage complacency and stagnation, and encourage routine brainstorming. We need to unlock their hidden brilliance by communicating this theme over and over, holding regular brainstorming sessions, and rewarding big ideas and smart risk-taking. Our followers will lead

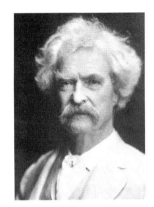

Mark Twain

us to the risks we should take. But to be first, we first need to ask them to innovate, and then we need to listen. So, as part of your plan to become a better risk taker, I recommend that you also implement some of these suggestions with your followers.

Guard Against Dumb Risks

In our zeal to improve risk-taking, we must still guard against excessive risks. One important aspect of that is making sure that people are not able to take actions that put others at risk without also putting themselves at risk. Let me explain. In recent years, Wall Street has come under attack because various bank executives took extraordinary risks that did not pan out. As a result, shareholders lost money, and taxpayers, in many cases, had to foot the bill. More often than not, however,

7

executives who made the poor decisions still made out like banshees. What on earth were they thinking? Well, it's quite simple. According to many analysts, executives took excessive risk because doing so posed little risk to them personally. They put long-term shareholder value at risk, took big pay in the meantime, and figured that if the risk ever materialized into a wide-scale real estate bubble, the government would rescue them. They were right.

The inherent problem was poor risk alignment. If you are in a position that allows you to influence incentives, please take it seriously. To the extent possible, make sure that those who are able to take big risks have an equally big stake in the outcomes– that they cannot take risks to benefit themselves but jeopardize others.

Reflections

Risk is tricky business. Some say stick to the facts. Others say go with your gut. I recommend a combination approach. Think through your risk-taking opportunities by carefully calculating the likelihood and magnitude of the upside and downside of both action and inaction. Then apply your best judgment, listen to your gut and make the best decision you can at the time. Prepare in advance for course corrections due to mistake or failure. Learn from mistakes, and don't hesitate in changing direction. This approach will give you the confidence to take more smart risks than your peers and competitors, creating more change and more progress.

Start applying this approach one risk at a time. Move from zero to something and then build. While you're at it, take steps to instill a risk-taking, innovation culture where you work. Here are some additional reflective questions to help get you started:

7

1) What are your current tendencies when it comes to taking risks?

2) How do you currently assess the risk of various opportunities?

3) How does your risk tolerance compare with your organization's risk tolerance?

4) What are your superiors' expectations with regard to risk-taking?

5) What are examples of smart risks and dumb risks you have encountered?

6) What's a risky decision you face now, at work and/or in your personal life?

7) How can you reduce or eliminate some of the fallout from a risk that doesn't pan out?

8) What prevents you from taking risks sometimes? Is it fear of rejection? A need for approval? The need to always be right? Fear of hurting others? The need to avoid guilt? A lack of belief in yourself or others? A desire to avoid conflict? The need to understand every detail? Denial that change is needed or even possible? A belief that it's not your problem? Are you more focused on your image and reputation than what you want to accomplish?

9) In what ways do you manage risk, and in what ways sometimes does risk manage you?

10) In your current role(s), how will the levels of risk you are willing or unwilling to accept impact the results you are trying to produce?

Relentless: *Unyielding, sustained pace or intensity; steady; persistent.*

Resolve: *Firmness of purpose or intent; determination.*

The world is full of talent, potential, good ideas, and good intentions. But success remains the rare bird. Too often, talent is squandered, potential is unrealized, ideas never get wings, and good intentions lose out to laziness.

Success requires something more.

The same can be said when looking at the R's of Leadership. We can focus on **Results** by establishing a clear vision and goals, effective execution strategies and meaningful measurement methods. We can be firmly grounded in **Reality**. We can have all the proper **Resources**. We can establish clear and effective **Rules, Roles** and **Responsibilities**. We can foster **Respectful Relationships**. We can take risks and establish a culture of smart **Risk-taking**. We can take time for **Recovery** from job stresses and establish a healthy work/life balance. We can provide **Recognition** to people and their positive contributions. We can practice **Reflective thinking**. And, guess what? We can still fail!

Success requires something more.

The missing ingredient, of course, is the title of this chapter: **Relentless Resolve**. You might want to think of it as an intangible. It's not something we do, so much as something we display.

Harvey MacKay, a prominent businessman and author, wrote in one of his nationally syndicated columns that *"it isn't the quality of the ideas you have that will determine whether you are successful, it's the qualities you bring to those ideas."* I would expand that to say success depends on the qualities we bring to all aspects of our pursuits, not just to our ideas. And the greatest of those qualities is Relentless Resolve. It is that "something more" that binds all of the ingredients to success.

Never Quit!

My sister, Tori, has always been a great example of someone with relentless resolve. She was still in high school when she first started defying the time management gods by working full-time. It wasn't because our parents pressured her. She simply wanted to go to college, and that required saving some money. Her dream was to get a degree and then start both a career and family. This was back before it was common for women to work double-time as moms and career professionals. But even back then, she wanted it all. And she was willing to do whatever it took to get it. I remember times when she would hold down three jobs at once, and I would quietly marvel at

Never Quit!

her determination. I remember when she got married and no longer "needed" to work (at least not to make ends meet), but she did so anyway because that was her vision for herself. She has truly been a remarkable influence, never more than when her husband began to die and she became his caretaker. At a time when others may have crumbled under the emotional and mental weight of the situation, she managed to put her all into making his last year as pleasant and love-filled as possible. Again, I marveled. She was so resilient (another favorite 'R' quality). When she made up her mind to do something, she always did it, regardless of the odds or obstacles. She suffered setbacks, like we all do. But she never let it deter her. She was relentless. She showed resolve. She never gave up!

I've tried to emulate her in that regard, living quite visibly by the mantra "Never Quit." In fact, my license plates have read "NVRQUIT" for years. It's a mindset that served me well in the military, especially on multi-day training hikes with 100 pounds on my back, or on stressful missions. It helped when I established my first corporate university in the face of strong resistance from existing training teams who saw no reason to fold their work into a new entity. The Never Quit mindset helped when I led my first sales organization and once again

8

met strong resistance from employees who saw me as an out-sider who simply didn't understand. It helped when I led my first manufacturing organization and was challenged to pro-duce results that seemed unrealistic. It helped when, after a cor-porate reorganization that divided HR responsibilities, I end-ed up with less influence than I had previously held. It helped when I was five hours into my first Ironman triathlon and real-ized I still wasn't halfway to the finish line. It also helped when I moved to a new job with a new company and found that the pace and demands of work far surpassed what I had expected.

Yes, I have wanted to quit many times. But I never do. That's not to say I haven't changed course. Trust me, I have left jobs, I have left relationships, and I have altered plans that weren't working. But when I do, it's never because things are tough; it's because the relentless pursuit of my goals requires the change.

It's one thing to leave an unhappy marriage, for example, and quite another thing to give up on marriage altogether, if a happy marriage is your goal. Likewise, it's one thing to aban-don a particular strategy for increasing sales, and quite anoth-er to give up on the possibility of increasing sales.

It can be a fine line, I understand. But we as leaders need to stick to our guns and always do what we feel is the next right thing. We can't be swayed by political winds or office relationships. We can't be deterred by short-term setbacks or even colossal failures. It's OK to switch gears, but we need to keep driving toward the destination. We're in charge of busi-ness plans, strategies and visions. These are not small matters. They are big things that require time and will no doubt chal-lenge our ability to deal with adversity and overcome failure. Expect such challenges. And face them head on. Fly the relent-less resolve flag, and never give up!

8

Giving Up v. Settling

There's more to relentless resolve than never giving up. It's also about not settling for less than you expect. If there is one thing I have seen as a common failure of leadership in my lifetime, it is this notion of "settling" or "compromising." Now, don't get me wrong: I don't think compromise is the dirty word that some make it out to be. Compromise reflects teamwork and – let's be honest – it gets things done, even if only in piecemeal fashion. Often times, it gets you from zero to something! But I would argue that settling and compromise should remain steps along the path to your goals, not end points.

For example, if your team is simply not talented or educated enough to meet your big goals, don't settle for doing the best you can with the people you have. You may have to do that in the short term, but don't compromise your ultimate goals. You may have to spend more time than you envisioned training and developing your team. You might have to allow people to fail at meeting your expectations and then upgrade your talent every time someone leaves or is terminated. You may have to do lots of things. And it may take time. But you don't have to settle for a B when you're aiming for an A – not long-term anyway.

It's worth reiterating: you may need and want to settle for B's along the way in order to make consistent progress, but you don't have to compromise the goal of earning an A in the end, even if everyone else seems happy with a B, including your bosses. See, that's the danger: consistently setting goals and then settling for what you get, rather than what you wanted. I saw this time and time again at The Schwan Food Company. Salespeople would aim for the highest sales club but then would put forth a normal, comfortable amount of effort and fall short. They would often achieve enough to keep their bosses reasonably happy, but they would rarely meet their goals. It became a pattern in which goals were rendered meaningless, except to those few who would do all the little things to demonstrate relentless resolve – little things like asking customers for referrals, carrying product to customers' doors to facilitate up-sales, introducing the service to some customers' neighbors each day, comparison shopping at local grocery stores, etc. Only the best had the resolve and were relentless enough to work smart day in and day out. Only the best did whatever it took to meet their goals. Only the best refused to settle for less.

I differentiate the "settling" or "compromising" scenario from the "giving up" scenario because in my mind, giving up means something much less than earning an A or B; it means dropping the class, so to speak. When the going gets tough, we have three options: abandon the goal (give up), lower the acceptable standard (settle) or plow ahead smartly (demonstrate relentless resolve). My experience is that, for most of us, settling is a much more realistic danger than giving up altogether.

All-Out Commitment

Relentless resolve springs from commitment, which John C. Maxwell explored in his fantastic book "The 21 Indispensable Qualities of a Leader." In it, he describes four types of people, in terms of commitment:

1) **Cop outs** – People who have no goals and do not commit.

2) **Holdouts** – People who don't know if they can reach their goals, so they're afraid to commit.

3) **Dropouts** – People who start toward a goal but quit or settle for less when the effort gets particularly difficult.

4) **All-outs** – People who set goals, commit to them and pay the price to reach them.

Obviously, the idea is to pursue our dreams and goals all-out. But, "At what price?" What price are we willing to pay for our goals? Many of us have lots of "goals" that compete with one another for our time and energy. Is it possible to go all-out for all of them? Maybe not. But the whole exercise of thinking about it can be a valuable way of prioritizing so that you only commit to those goals you are truly able and willing to pursue all-out.

Prioritizing Commitments

Indeed, prioritizing your ambition is a necessary step, because achieving your biggest goals usually requires sacrificing some of your smaller goals. Prioritizing, then, puts you in position to demonstrate relentless resolve. To use a simple example: if one of my big goals is to complete an Ironman triathlon, I may need to set aside or delay goals that involve golf, reading, learning the piano, traveling, etc. I may even need to alter my work and family goals in some way, simply because of the time it will take me to train. I have  found that most people can manage three major commitments simultaneously (e.g. work, parenting, training for marathon). But once you try to manage four or more big goals or commitments, your ability to go all-out for all of them diminishes. So,

8

prioritize and commit carefully or you may handicap your ability to apply relentless resolve.

Prioritizing Areas of Focus

Another type of priority, beyond specific goals or commitments, is the kind that represents the general way we prefer to go about our life and business. For example, here are three of my steadfast work priorities, aka areas of focus, that I try to pursue with relentless resolve.

1) I think it's important to be relentless about **execution and accountability**. This goes back to Chapter 1 and using the right metrics. It's hard to know if our employees are executing the strategy unless we have concrete ways of measuring individual and team performance. It's been said: "What gets measured gets done." I believe that 100 percent. But metrics alone aren't enough. As leaders, we need to actually check the measurements, too, and hold people accountable to them.

   I don't necessarily believe we need to spend inordinate amounts of time checking up on every detail of every employee. But all employees need to understand we are watching the metrics, and they need to know their work could be noticed and reviewed, for better and worse, at any time. Over time, you will learn who on your team is independently accountable and who needs more supervision and monitoring. What's critical, for me, is to be relentless about having good metrics and checking them often enough to hold people accountable and ensure execution. Complacency in this area is a recipe for failure.

2) I also try to relentlessly adhere to **my values**. I've already talked about doing the "next right thing," which is a slogan

borrowed from the book Alcoholics Anonymous.

A variation, which may or may not be attributable to me ☺, is to do the "hard right thing." It's a slogan acknowledging that the right decision is often the hard decision, but the one I need to make. It's about remaining ruthlessly true to my beliefs and never compromising my integrity. This is critical because my integrity is the primary source of my personal power and influence as a leader.

The cost of being true to oneself is sometimes popularity. As leaders, we are bound to upset some people, and we won't always be liked. But that's just part of the leadership gig. In the end, it's respect from self and others that we really seek. Relentlessly guarding our values and beliefs is a testament to our character, attracting respect from even those who disagree. When faced with making a potentially unpopular decision, I ease my own mind by answering questions such as: Does my decision feel right? Is it reasonable? Does it pass the "red face" test, meaning, could I explain it to my mother without getting embarrassed or feeling ashamed? When the answers are yes, my resolve hardens, making it much easier to move forward and accept any resulting negative feedback.

3) Finally, I also am committed to relentlessly **training, educating and developing my team** members. To me, it's a must. We can't expect people to simply figure things out, unless of course we're willing to suffer the organizational pains when they struggle and risk the possibility they will never figure things out to our liking. In my mind, that is unnecessary and unacceptable. We also can't rely exclusively on people developing themselves

unless we're willing to replace them when they don't. I firmly believe it's more cost-effective, not to mention more employee friendly, to invest proactively in training, education and ongoing development. It will always be a professional priority that I pursue relentlessly.

Progress, Not Perfection

The organization Alcoholics Anonymous has another wise old slogan about the value of pursuing progress rather than perfection. And when you think about it, that turn of phrase really embodies the whole "Zero to Something" philosophy. I think it's particularly relevant in this chapter. After all, what is it that generally challenges our resolve? Setbacks. Mistakes. Failures. Imperfection.

In the previous chapter on risk-taking, I discussed not fearing failure and failing fast. Here, too, it's important to highlight the inevitability, as well as the natural value, of falling short.

As I write this, Elon Musk has helped found four different companies, each worth billions of dollars – the online payment services company PayPal, commercial space pioneer SpaceX, electric car pioneer Tesla, and energy company SolarCity.

Elon Musk

Mr. Musk is no stranger to taking risks, having leveraged most of his personal fortune to get SpaceX off the ground. He's also no stranger to failure. After four years designing and developing the Falcon-1 rocket in the early 2000s, SpaceX spent the next three years trying to launch it into orbit. Three times, it failed. And by that time, as I mentioned, Mr. Musk's own fortune was almost gone.

8

He figured he had enough money for just one more attempt. Asked if he was optimistic, he uttered the famous quote below.

> *"Optimism, pessimism, f**k that; we're going to make it happen. As God is my bloody witness, I'm hell-bent on making it work."* – *entrepreneur Elon Musk*

It was the epitome of going all-out, of demonstrating relentlessness and resolve. He was "hell-bent" on making it work. Sure enough, on the fourth try, in 2008, it did work. And a year later, the rocket carried a Malaysian satellite into orbit for a fee, making it the first privately financed vehicle to take a commercial payload into space. SpaceX is now doing NASA-like work at about 10% of the production cost, according to some reports. In 2012, SpaceX used its Dragon spacecraft to become the first private company to carry a commercial payload to the International Space Station. But it's important to understand that, for Mr. Musk, today's success is built on yesterday's failures.

With each setback, Musk had the opportunity to bail on the venture or change the goal. But instead, he allowed his company to learn from each mistake and to make consistent progress toward the goal. While he may have hoped for perfection from the get-go, it certainly wasn't expected. He did expect progress, though, and he was relentless about achieving the ultimate goal.

When you're struggling, it's not easy to remain hell-bent and to demonstrate resolve. After thousands of failed attempts at inventing the light bulb, it probably wasn't easy for Thomas Edison to keep trying new filaments. But he did. And, eventually, there was light!

"Many of life's failures are people who did not realize how close they were to success when they gave up."
– inventor Thomas Edison

According to Edison, we need to figure out what doesn't work before we can know what does work. It seems so intuitive. But, as we know, it's so easy to forget. We always seem to want to nail things on the first try.

The next time you're reeling from a setback, allow yourself to be inspired by stories such as Edison's and Musk's. Then go ahead and write your own story of progress, not perfection.

Love the Long-Term

What helps me overcome failure is to keep thinking long-term. A bad workout, for example, does not mean I will not reach my goal of completing an upcoming race. And a bad race does not mean I won't have a good race the next time or that I am not achieving good health. Likewise, a lackluster presentation at work does not mean I won't help the department achieve its goals. Even missing an annual goal does not mean we'll miss our three-year goal or that we're not making progress on our vision and strategy.

The long-term mindset may be most difficult to maintain during the so-called "flat period." That's the time at the beginning of a business or project when your effort is great but the gains are slight. It's when you are setting the table for success, making the small changes that eventually will reach a critical mass and produce big gains, but which haven't produced those gains yet. Businesses aren't generally profitable right away. And struggling professional sports teams don't usually rebuild overnight. They all go through a flat period as they lay the groundwork for success. It takes time, for example, for people to fully understand what you want them to accomplish, how you want them to accomplish it, and what's in it for them.

Do yourself a favor: expect a flat period. Expect, as I mentioned, setbacks and outright failures. Expect criticism and even a lack of support from others. But don't give up or compromise your goal simply because the gains aren't coming fast enough. Through it all, maintain an intelligent long-term outlook. Learn at every juncture, and stick to the plan with relentless resolve.

The key, as we've said all along, is to consistently make progress. When we do that, goals have a way of getting met, and usually sooner than later. In this sense, the "Zero to Something" philosophy is a sensible bridge between short- and long-term thinking – a call for short-term progress but long-term results. It's the kind of philosophy that attracts investors.

> *"Time is the friend of the wonderful company, the enemy of the mediocre." – legendary investor Warren Buffett, chairman of Berkshire Hathaway*

Next Steps

To begin applying the concepts of this chapter, first think about one of your greatest accomplishments – something that required work to achieve and brought you great pride. Then, ask your-

8

self: How did I do that? Was it a specific goal of mine? What qualities did I bring to it? What mistakes or setbacks did I suffer along the way? How did I respond to them? Was I ever tempted to give up or settle for less? Why didn't I? What price did I pay for this achievement? Did I have to prioritize my commitments to succeed? What were my competing commitments? In what ways was I "all out" or "hell-bent?" Did I have a "short-term progress/long-term results" mindset?

Next, I would like you to follow the recommendation of leadership consultant and executive coach Doug Sundheim:

1) Pick some area of your life where you are dissatisfied with your progress or results. Write it down.

2) Answer this question on paper and out loud: "If I were hell-bent on getting the results I want, what would I do differently than I'm doing now?"

3) Then finish this sentence on paper and out loud: "If in six months, I'm not getting the progress or results I want, the reasons will be ..."

4) Start doing the things you wrote in #2 and preventing or avoiding the things you wrote in #3.

5) Repeat relentlessly and with resolve, as necessary.

Applying this approach to a single area of your life will help you go from zero to something. The idea is to begin recognizing what it takes to rise above the rest of the leadership pack and to recognize your own ability to go all out. After meeting this first identified goal or objective, you will be primed to move on to the next one and succeed once again.

Reflections

What I have found is that relentless resolve is less about taking extraordinary measures and more about consistently doing the little things that make a difference, even when the little things go unnoticed. It's about prioritizing in a way that allows you to invest fully. And most importantly, it's about maintaining a stick-to-it attitude when setbacks and challenges inevitably arise.

I think it's useful to assume that the leaders with whom you compete are working relentlessly to outperform you. That is absolutely true of your highest performing peers. But the reality is that most leaders are not so relentless and resolute. Most do not have the discipline to do the important little things day

> ## "Relentless Resolve is something that will set you apart from most of your peers."

in and day out. Most do not narrow their commitments enough to devote themselves completely. And most shrink when the going gets tough. Relentless resolve is something that will set you apart from most of your peers. And it's absolutely necessary if you aim to compete with the best of the best in your chosen field.

Here are a few reflective questions to get you thinking more about this critical aspect of leadership:

1) How might your own relentless resolve, or lack thereof, impact your team members?

2) What's the difference between relentless resolve and wasted effort?

3) Do you have a project that you gave up on that should be re-started? Explain.

4) Do you have a project that caused you to settle for less, but that in retrospect could have been pursued more relentlessly and resolutely? Explain.

5) Do you remember a time when you were so relentless you beat the proverbial "dead horse" and should have instead altered course and pursued the same goal by other means? Explain.

6) What commitments are you currently juggling, and what opportunity is there to narrow your commitments so you can invest more in your biggest priorities?

7) What price are you willing to pay to meet your biggest goals?

8) What does "progress, not perfection" mean to you?

9) What barriers are there to maintaining a long-term mindset, and how can you overcome them?

10) What would it mean to relentlessly pursue the R's of Leadership?

8

11) How can you set aside cynicism and allow yourself to be inspired by others who have demonstrated relentless resolve?

Recovery: *The act of restoring or returning to a better, healthier condition.*

It is true that good leaders get the most out of themselves and their teams. The question, of course, is how. For years, even generations, the simple answer was to demand more. It was based on this thinking: the more you ask of people, the more you will receive. Even today, this notion resonates. Leaders can get a long way by setting high expectations and maintaining firm accountability (i.e. demanding more). But, it is clear now that such thinking oversimplifies the human performance equation and, as a result, limits a leader's potential. That is why so much more has been written on the topic of leadership and performance improvement during the past 50 years. We've learned there's more to it!

In this book, I aim to condense and simplify that wide body of knowledge by sharing a framework that has proven useful to me. It would be disingenuous and nothing more than a marketing ploy to reduce leadership to a single concept. So, in the end, I leave you with 11 R's to support my "zero to something" philosophy. Like the famous guitar amplifier in the rock 'n' roll spoof, *This is Spinal Tap*, my list is better than top-10 lists because, well, it "goes to 11." Seriously, though, I hope the odd number and the comprehensive nature of this book do signify that *Zero to Something* is intended to be practical and that it's a genuine representation of my leadership approach – not a slick, manufactured attempt to capitalize on the desire for a quick fix.

It is in that context that I introduce this chapter's R – Recovery. On the one hand, the message is simple: there is more to life than work, so take care of yourself and encourage your team members to do the same. On the other hand, it's complex because it's so much easier said than done. But why? What makes it so?

In my view, many of us just aren't sure recovery is necessary, or that it's possible. We view it as nice to have, but not needed. In our minds, it is subservient to the concepts of hard work and relentless resolve. No doubt, in the United States, our capitalist culture plays a role. Hard work is at the heart of the so-called American Dream, after all. And, in many lives – mine included – hard work almost always pays off to some degree. But, if we want to be more effective than the average leaders, we need to realize there's more to human performance than hard work and more to leading people than simply squeezing additional time and energy out of them. We need to take advantage of the new knowledge that makes it clear: hard work, unbridled, has diminishing returns. We cannot expect relentlessness without rest.

9

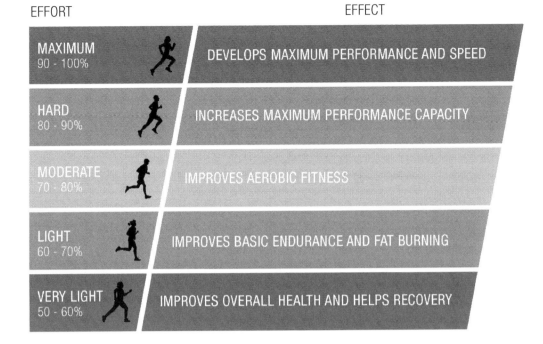

EFFORT		EFFECT
MAXIMUM 90 - 100%		DEVELOPS MAXIMUM PERFORMANCE AND SPEED
HARD 80 - 90%		INCREASES MAXIMUM PERFORMANCE CAPACITY
MODERATE 70 - 80%		IMPROVES AEROBIC FITNESS
LIGHT 60 - 70%		IMPROVES BASIC ENDURANCE AND FAT BURNING
VERY LIGHT 50 - 60%		IMPROVES OVERALL HEALTH AND HELPS RECOVERY

I see this especially clearly in my hobby as a triathlete. Just a generation ago, training was simple: log more miles on the road and more laps in the pool. It's a strategy that produced results. But, eventually, as athletes sought ways to gain an edge on the competition, and as science advanced, we learned how to train better, not just harder. We learned, for example, that training at various speeds and distances stresses the heart and muscles more effectively than simply running longer and longer distances. As such, many athletes go into workouts today monitoring heart rate and duration but paying little mind to distance. That's quite a sea change to the concept of simply logging more miles. More significantly, at least to our topic here, we also have learned that muscles actually grow and adapt to hard work after the workout, when they're resting and regenerating. So, to train incessantly is to stress already stressed muscles. Today, the best athletes are very strategic and purposeful about including rest days and light workouts (active recovery days) in their training schedules. It's not about relaxing or getting a break. It's about maximizing their strength and speed gains. To them, training any other way would be stupid.

Somehow, this concept has not resonated so clearly in the business world. We pay a lot of lip service to the need for regular recovery. But, when push comes to shove, it's often the first thing to go, which means it's no strategy at all, but rather a nice-to-have benefit. I submit that if we think of it differently – strategically, like an athlete – we will gain an advantage over other leaders, many of whom remain stuck in the concepts of yesterday.

The Facts

• 89 percent of Americans say work/life balance is a problem in the United States, and, of those, 57 percent say it's a significant problem, according to an August 2010 survey by StrategyOne.

• America's No. 1 health problem is stress, and "job stress is the major culprit," according to the American Institute of Stress.

• In a 2006 survey by ComPsych, an employee assistance program provider, 46 percent of respondents said workload was the main cause of stress in their lives; 20 percent attributed their primary stress to "juggling work/personal lives;" and 6 percent attributed their main stress to lack of job security. In total, 72 percent reported work-related stress causes, while only 28 percent reported personal issues as their main cause of stress.

• A 2005 study by the Family and Work Institute found that 33 percent of American employees are chronically overworked and that 54 percent felt overwhelmed in the past month by workload.

• A 2006 survey by the Randstad Group found that 57 percent of Generation Y employees and 26 percent of Baby Boomers deal with stress by taking off unplanned days from work.

• The Bureau of Labor Statistics estimates that people who take time off from work for stress, anxiety or related disorders miss an average of 20 days.

• Health care expenditures are nearly 50% greater for workers who report high levels of stress, according to a 1998 study published in the *Journal of Occupational and Environmental Medicine.*

• The American Institute on Stress estimates that stress-related issues – i.e. absenteeism, burnout, mental health issues, lower productivity, diminished customer service – cost American businesses $300 billion annually.

• According to many studies, an increasing percentage of employees value work/life balance above all other job attributes, including money, advancement potential and location.

I am willing to bet these statistics – to one degree or another – jive with your own feelings, experiences and observations related to work stress and work/life balance. We all know it's a problem. The bigger problem, however, is that we generally accept being overwhelmed with work as a fact of life. If anything, we feel guilty when we rest. My question is, why? And, how? How can we accept the preventable costs noted above as a fact of life? Would a serious athlete acknowledge that recovery time makes her faster but neglect it anyway for the false pleasure of training hard every day? No, it would be delusional. Yet, that is exactly what we do when we drive our teams and ourselves to a never-ending brink, failing to make planned recovery a part of our strategy.

> *"It seems that we have it backward in our society. We tend to look up to people who are under a great deal of stress."* – <u>Don't Sweat the Small Stuff</u> *by Richard Carlson, Ph.D.*

Signs of Stress

One of the first steps for us, as leaders, is to learn how to recognize stress so that we know when recovery is needed. We cannot treat people like dogs and run them ragged (ourselves included). In many ways, our canine friends are the ultimate recovery machines, famous for going until they cannot go anymore, and then crashing to recover and eventually coming back to full strength. But the problem in drawing a parallel to humans is that people cannot afford to run to the point of exhaustion – mainly because we don't have the luxury of being able to crash long enough for a full recovery; in most cases, we still need to keep working, parenting, paying the bills, etc. So, wait-

ing for a natural crash is impractical. Instead, we must manage stress and performance simultaneously, and recognize how one affects the other. While it's probably not feasible to measure stress as closely or accurately as we measure performance, it's still important to be on the lookout for the telltale signs of stress and long-term burnout.

First, think about how you feel when particularly stressed. You probably feel like you cannot keep up with everything you need to do. You probably feel some difficulty in balancing your work demands with family, friends, non-work interests and the normal chores of everyday living. As a result, you may struggle with setting priorities and limits, which may lead to feelings of helplessness and self-doubt. After a while of feeling overwhelmed and perhaps falling short in one or more areas of your life, you might get to the point of not caring so much about work, content to simply get by rather than to exert influence. Or, you might neglect some other important area of your life. Either way, you probably feel some sense of failure and dissatisfaction. Or, you might just keep pushing until you're "dog-tired," and that's when you start missing work, getting in accidents, and/or requiring health care, costing your employer money, as the previously noted statistics attest. At some point, time off from work may no longer even provide any sense of renewal. Does any of that sound familiar? Well, whether you have experienced any of those symptoms and stages of stress or not, it's a pretty typical description of what goes through the mind of a stressed employee. So, be aware of such feelings in yourself.

It's a little more difficult to monitor your team members' thoughts and feelings because they won't always share them freely. People are proud. And, even though there's nothing weak about reaching one's limits, it is human nature to deny such realities. As leaders, we cannot wait for our team members to "cry uncle." We need to look for the external signs of stress and burnout. Indeed, we may be able to see the signs even before our team members recognize the symptoms in themselves.

- Increased fatigue – physical, mental or emotional
- Increased headaches, pains and sickness
- Withdrawal from coworkers and projects (isolation)
- Less attention to responsibilities
- Increased substance use and abuse (tobacco, alcohol, drugs)
- Significant weight gain or loss
- Increased tardiness (sometimes combined with shorter workdays)
- Increased absenteeism
- Increased anger, irritability and hostility
- Increased sadness, gloom and dejection
- Increased negativity, pessimism and cynicism
- Decreased confidence and self-esteem
- Decreased motivation and/or ambition
- Compromised ideals and/or integrity
- Decreased productivity
- Increased procrastination
- Decreased work quality
- Increased complaints from co-workers

The key is to look for *changes*. For example, if someone's work quality is lower than a peer's, that does not necessarily mean the employee is overworked. Obviously. However, if someone once had a higher work quality that has dropped noticeably (whether suddenly or over time), then that might be a sign of stress, particularly if it's accompanied by other changes in behavior or attitude. Sometimes, the changes may even be counter-intuitive. For example, some people respond to stress, at least initially, by getting more engaged – even over-engaged. Such folks will take on more work, seek out more projects and put in more hours in an attempt to gain or regain control. In fact, this is often the scenario that plays out before the more telltale symptoms listed above take hold. Again, it's most important to look into changes you see – *changes* of any kind.

> *"Too much work and too much energy kill a man just as effectively as too much assorted vice or too much drink."*
> *– author Rudyard Kipling*

I think you'll find that those who burn out the most are often the same people who show the most promise at the start of their careers – idealists and achievers with high energy, positive attitudes, dedication and commitment. Unfortunately, as they demonstrate more ability and seek out more responsibility, more and more work gets shuffled their way. Over time, the relentless pace and demands outpace their ability to cope, and burnout ensues. Our job, then, if we are to be better than the average leader, is to see signs of stress and manage them so that employees never suffer burnout and can perform optimally for themselves and for us at all times.

Funkytown

When thinking about my own stress or coaching others, I often use a metaphor based on a fictional place I call Funkytown. Despite the fun vibe of the hit song with the same name, (by Lipps Inc.), Funkytown is not a place you want to be. It's a lonely town where everything is dark and colorless. When I start to feel funky (or breathless, as my colleague and friend, Amy Lenert once described it) – when I'm stressed, tired, sick or otherwise off my game – I imagine heading down the highway, getting closer and closer to Funkytown and watching as my surroundings transition from Technicolor to black and white.

The imagery makes it easier for me to envision turning around. It reminds me that I do not *have* to feel that way and that my current destination is not where I normally reside.

It empowers me to apply the brakes and think about what I need to do to change course. Sometimes, I need extra sleep. Or exercise. Or I need more time with my family, or more time with myself.

Sometimes, I just need to talk with others. In any case, the key is recognizing the need for recovery. When I'm headed for Funkytown, and not yet aware of it, it's another example of playing blind. Because my situational awareness is low, my decision quality is compromised, rendering me unconsciously incompetent. Getting a glimpse of the black-and-white road sign for Funkytown instantly improves my situational awareness and decision quality, and it allows me to start considering what's needed for a u-turn.

Even so, there are times when we all end up passing the road sign and venturing into Funkytown. If that starts to happen frequently, though, it's time to take an even deeper breath and look around at the causes. There's nothing good about accumulating reward points at the dank Funkytown Motel!

What I like about the Funkytown metaphor is that it's vivid and memorable. As such, it has proven valuable to those I lead and coach, as well as to me.

Causes of Stress

Now that we know what to look for, let's take a look at the causes of work stress, which will drive the solutions we consider in the next section. I've already alluded to overworking as a cause of stress, but that is certainly not the only one. Here are the ones I've found to be most prominent, in no particular order.

- High work volume (too many responsibilities; unrealistic expectations; information overload)

- High work frequency (lengthy days and/or weeks; not enough time off)

- High work intensity (overly demanding – physically, mentally and/or emotionally), i.e. high-pressure or chaotic environment; high levels of interpersonal conflict, etc.

- Feeling undervalued; lack of acknowledgement, recognition and reward for good work

- Absence of clear milestones; no end point(s) to one's efforts

- Lack of control over one's work

- Lack of close, supportive relationships with leaders and/or peers

- Unclear job expectations; conflicting demands

- Too much higher-up bureaucracy with which to contend

9

- Fear of layoffs during down economy
  (personal finance pressures)

- Reluctance to delegate to others or say 'no'

- Perfectionism (leading one to think nothing is ever
  good enough)

- Boring and/or unfulfilling work

- Consistently inadequate sleep and/or poor nutrition
  (which change hormone levels that negatively affect
  stress tolerance, muscle recovery and mood)

- Value conflicts with organization

Recovery Solutions

As you can see, the stress causes listed above go way beyond workload, to include work environment, work processes, individual personality traits, etc. As such, we can minimize a good deal of our team members' stress simply by pursuing good general leadership principles. For example, as leaders, we should establish a culture in which people feel valued, acknowledged, recognized and rewarded (see Chapter 10 on Recognition). We should establish clear milestones and celebrate them (see Chapter 1 on Results). We should empower people to influence their own work and work processes (see Chapter 5 on Roles & Responsibilities and Chapter 7 on Risk Taking). We should provide adequate support for people (see Chapter 3 on Resources) and cultivate teamwork (see Chapter 6 on Respectful Relationships). We should limit frustrating red tape (see Chapter 4 on

9

Rules). We should create clear and reasonable expectations (see Chapter 1 on Results). We should talk to our team members about their fears and desires for work fulfillment, coach them on skills such as delegation and managing perfectionism, and even discuss away-from-work issues such as sleep (see Chapter 5 on Roles & Responsibilities and Chapter 6 on Respectful Relationships). We also should create an atmosphere where team members feel free to discuss value conflicts (see Chapter 2 on Reality).

Yes, a lot of stress management comes down to being the leader your team or organization needs, focused on the R's of Leadership and the "Zero to Something" mindset. But people who work for strong leaders will undoubtedly experience stress as well – from the relentless pursuit of consistent progress, if nothing else. So, strategies aimed directly at recovering from the volume, frequency and intensity of workloads are important, too, and that's what I'd like to focus on here.

Let's establish three important facts up front.

1) To be sure, we cannot expect to prevent or eliminate ALL work stress. Stress is a part of life. We can, however, strive to manage stress so that it does not negatively impact work performance.

2) Work/life balance is different for everyone. Solutions may look very different for a young, single employee than for a young, married mother of two. Work/life solutions may also vary based on the type of work people do. For example, someone working on an assembly line may have different work/life needs than a salesperson who travels a lot. It's a mistake to develop a single set of policies and

programs and expect them to magically solve everyone's work/life problems. One size does not fit all. We need flexibility in dealing with such issues.

3) We, as leaders, set the tone for recovery. If we model a poor work/life balance, others will feel compelled to follow. If we model a healthy work/life balance, others will be inclined to find their own balance. Consider the simple example of a leader who sends team members e-mails at 3 a.m., or who floods them with e-mails on the weekend, or who sends e-mails and participates in conference calls throughout vacation. This may initially make a leader proud – a way of showing your team members that you're willing to work hard, too. You might think it models relentless resolve. And, at times, that type of modeling may be beneficial, particularly in dealing with matters of genuine urgency. But if it's consistent and constant (i.e. people joke about you never sleeping), then you are not modeling the right balance. And, trust me, others will surely mimic your lack of balance. It's better to show them you can be relentless about both working and not working. Making balance a priority will not only keep you healthy and help you perform better over the long haul, but it will also encourage your team to do the same.

What is recovery?

Recovery, in my mind, involves two things: 1) HEALING: recharging yourself and your team after periods of intense activity and/or stress; and 2) GROWTH: building a balance of fitness across all spectrums of your life to protect against the need for healing, and helping your team members do the same.

Healing

Healing is probably the most obvious aspect of recovery. As discussed earlier, people wear down occasionally and need time to recuperate, get stronger and sustain motivation for the job. Recovery time is when the body and mind adapt to the stress of work and grow stronger in anticipation of more stress to come. Recovery time allows us to replenish energy stores and repair frayed nerves and muscles. Without sufficient time to repair and replenish, the body and mind continue to break down. But an effective alternation of adaptation and recovery will ultimately take you to a higher level of work fitness.

It is prudent to plan recovery periods for entire teams after long and/or intense projects. What does that mean? It could mean waiting to start the next project until the existing project is done. It could mean ramping up the intensity of the next project so that it doesn't start at the same level where the last one left off. It could mean rotating team members from more intense projects to less intense projects. It could mean planning, from the beginning, a week of "catch-up" at the end of intense projects. Those are just a few ideas. You probably have more.

As noted, different people will have different recovery needs, even if they're working on the same project, so it's also important to respond to team members' individual needs. Encourage people to plan and take vacations, especially if it seems they need one. Ask them to go home at the end of the day, especially when you're seeing negative signs of stress. Encourage and talk to them about hobbies and other non-work interests. Empower them to manage their time more efficiently. Be flexible with special requests, particularly those related to work schedules. Flexible work arrangements can relieve a lot of stress on two-income families with children, without compromising their ability to meet your expectations.

Understand that the greater the work intensity and effort, the greater the need for recovery. Understand also that some people are naturally more intense at work, regardless of the project, and may need more rest as a result. Folks also vary in terms of stress tolerance, non-work stress levels, nutrition, etc. Most important to us leaders, I believe, is to talk openly about recovery with our teams. Make them responsible for monitoring their own recuperative ability, and, at the same time, make it comfortable for them to voice individual recovery needs as they arise.

"Have fun in your command. Don't always run at a break-neck pace. Take leave when you've earned it: Spend time with your families. Corollary: surround yourself with people who take their work seriously, but not themselves, those who work hard and play hard." - Retired Gen. Colin Powell

I get that this may seem like "pie in the sky" to some of my readers. I realize that some of you believe employees will take a mile if given an inch. No doubt, some will. But, in my view, most won't. Respect begets respect. And I'd rather do what's best for my business and manage the exceptions than compromise my belief that appropriate recovery time produces more and better work over the long haul. As noted, I firmly believe, based on proven biological science, that, in many cases, an extra day of rest is more beneficial to the business than an extra day of work. If you're struggling with the concept, I encourage you to simply think about how your own body and mind respond to physical, mental and emotional stress. If you do, I'm confident you'll agree that recovery is not merely nice to have. It's an absolute necessity – something leaders should strategically plan for, pursue and protect.

Growth (in Fitness Levels)

Beyond helping team members heal from specific periods of high intensity, it's also important to help people grow healthier generally, to build stress tolerance. We can do this by modeling and promoting healthy work/life balance. I like to educate my teams about what I call the six "fitness levels:" physical fitness, mental and emotional fitness, spiritual fitness, family fitness, financial fitness, and professional fitness. In the end, don't you

Physical	Mental/ Emotional
Spiritual	Family
Financial $	Professional

agree that professional fitness (aka work fitness) can be jeopardized by troubles with other fitness levels? For example, if you are physically exhausted or emotionally drained, can that negatively affect your professional decision-making? The answer, obviously, is Yes. In fact, each fitness level has an impact on the others. So, our job as leaders is to promote total fitness. If professional fitness is pursued at the exclusion of the other fitness levels, total fitness will eventually collapse, and professional fitness will go down with the ship. By promoting total fitness – holistic health, as my yoga-instructor wife would say – we help to protect and actually improve professional fitness.

To explore the six fitness levels more, I'm going to pose some questions to help you consider your own fitness – the same kinds of questions you could discuss with your own team members.

1) **Physical** – What do you do to stay in shape? Do you have physical fitness goals? You don't need to run marathons or bench press 300 pounds to maintain physical health. But it is important to do some sort of cardiovascular workout three times a week for at least 30 minutes. It's also important to get sleep when you need it. Everybody requires different amounts of sleep, but studies show most people need six to 10 hours, with the average being eight. If you're getting less than six hours a night, it's probably too little. And if you need eight to function optimally, then even six or seven is too little. So figure out what you need to stay on top of your game and make getting that much sleep a priority. Finally, how is your nutrition? Are you at a healthy weight? Do you enjoy sugar in moderation? Do you eat fruits and vegetables? Do you see a primary care physician for annual physicals? Do you see a dentist every six months? Believe me, if you make physical fitness a priority, you will gain energy and feel better. Your mind will get better. And, your work will improve as well.

2) **Mental/Emotional** – Are you doing what's needed to stay in the "game" emotionally? Are you finding ways to continually learn and expand your mind? Do you have grief or trauma issues that may affect your emotional state? If so, are you seeing a therapist? Do you utilize your relationships by talking to others? The key here is to maintain the right frame of mind so you can do your job effectively. You want to be able to think clearly, without outside distractions. Don't car-

ry around anger, loneliness, resentments, depression, anxiety or other emotional baggage. You also want to be able to maintain healthy perspectives so you can stay focused on big, important things – not the small stuff.

3) **Spiritual** – Are you content spiritually? For some, spirituality is expressed and exercised by believing in god and attending church. However, for others, meditation or yoga may represent spirituality. For still others, spirituality may best be found in solitude at the top of a mountain, in a walk through the woods, or in a five-mile run. Most human beings have some conscious anxiety about the meaning of life and the uncertainty of death. That is why many of us seek spirituality – to help cope with life's grand questions, to gain some sense of our place in the universe, and to find a level of comfort with living. To live without spirituality or with fractured spirituality is, for some, to live with torment or yearning. If that's true for you, it is definitely worth investing some time and energy in exploring this aspect of your life.

4) **Family Fitness** – Are you making time to spend with your family? Are you taking care of their needs? Are you being the spouse, parent, sibling and son or daughter you want to be? Are you bringing family tensions with you to the workplace? Are you taking work stress home? All of this will get more challenging the farther you advance up the organizational chart. So, make it a priority. Continually seek balance, balance and more balance.

5) **Financial Fitness** – Are you saving money for the future? Have you established financial goals and a plan? Do you take advantage of every retirement planning opportunity that your employer provides? Are you over-extended? Are you

pre-occupied with issues of money? Do you have or need an advisor? It's not important to be rich, of course. But it is healthy to be free of significant concern.

6) **Professional Fitness** – What are you doing to develop yourself to meet the challenges of the future? Are you constantly upgrading yours skills, making sure you are well read and on the leading edge, rather than the bleeding edge, of leadership and your industry? Have you sat down and documented your leadership style, methods, and rationale? Do you have clear career goals? Are you progressing toward those goals? Are you succeeding in your current role? Are you staying relevant? In other words, are you still adding value?

Some Practical Tips for You and Your Team

- Start the day with a relaxing ritual. For example, spend 10 minutes meditating, stretching, writing in a journal, reading – whatever helps you begin the day in a healthy state of mind.

- Make time to get fresh air and see the sun throughout the day. Take a walk around the block during a break. Eat lunch outside. Etc.

- Make time to stretch occasionally throughout the day, whether at your work desk or elsewhere.

- Be choosey about your non-work commitments. It's OK to say no. Save your time for the commitments that mean the most to you.

- Take breaks from talking and technology, respectively. Perhaps you could eat lunch in silence every day and completely disconnect from your computer devices and phone at a certain time every evening.

- Explore your creativity. Engage in hobbies. Write. Sing. Play.

- Challenge yourself. Try new things at work and away from work, even when they're hard. Switch up your rou tines from time to time.

Another interesting thing you can do, now and then, is lead your team through some sort of time management or priorities exercise. For example, you could ask a series of questions designed to identify where team members spend their time in a typical 24 hours.

- How much time do you spend sleeping or trying to sleep?
- How much time do you spend preparing for work?
- How much time do you spend commuting to and from work?
- How much time do you spend working?
- How much time do you spend preparing and eating meals?
- How much time do you spend on errands and household chores?
- How much time do you spend caring for others?
- How much time do you spend on yourself?
- How does your "me time" correspond with the six fitness levels?

Often, the results of such an exercise surprise participants, who don't realize how little time they spend on their own total fitness. It becomes the starting point for a discussion about stress and recovery.

Next Steps

To me, the best way to start implementing this "R" is to define what work/life balance means to you and your team. Actually create and share a statement of some sort that indicates the goal of work/life balance is to achieve health and prosperity for both the organization and individual team members. It's important that the concept be seen as both an employee and organizational priority. And that statement cannot be seen as spin. If you believe what I've written here, it isn't spin. As I've described, work/life balance and recovery from work stress actually improve employee performance.

Next, with your statement as a foundation, develop a small set of guiding principles. Guiding principles might express respect for employees' time off, a commitment to flexibility, recognition and support for the six levels of total fitness, etc.

Example Statement and Guiding Principles:

Team X is committed to work/life balance as a means of achieving health and prosperity for both the organization and its employees.

1) Team X respects employees' time away from work as a healthy influence on their ability to contribute effectively at work.

2) Team X is committed to reasonable flexibility in helping the organization and its employees achieve work/life balance.

3) Team X promotes total fitness for its employees, which can include physical, mental/emotional, spiritual, family, financial and professional fitness.

This is as far or official as I would go with policy. Communicate these principles and use them to influence your decisions. But leave yourself the flexibility to deal with people's stress and recovery needs on an individual basis, in ways that benefit both employee and employer.

As you proceed under such a statement and guidelines, be sure to stay on constant lookout for signs of stress. Remember that you can alleviate a good deal of stress by simply leading effectively and implementing the various leadership R's. Make sure to model appropriate work/life balance yourself. Plan for recovery periods when team members are involved in particularly intense efforts. Educate team members about the fitness levels and create an environment in which work/life balance is actively promoted, examined and talked about.

Reflections

Looking back to my youth, a phrase that always stuck with me was "Taking A Timeout." In sports, I never associated timeouts with weakness. Having a timeout and using it was an advantage or strength. Unfortunately, at some point in my work life, taking a timeout became stigmatized. But the more I learn, the sillier that seems. Given the fast pace of today's world, it is more critical than ever to counter relentless work with relent-

less recovery, whether rest or play. Recovery is a natural process, like sleep, and it's an important part of our leadership responsibilities, as well as our own personal and professional development.

As you think more about this topic, consider these reflective questions:

1) What are my objectives around work/life balance, both for myself and for my team members? What outcomes do I seek?

2) What policies are in place regarding this topic?

3) What scares me about discussing this topic with team members?

4) What do I do now to recover from work? What do my team members do?

5) What am I doing this week or next week to recover?

6) What relaxes me? Do I do it enough?

7) How many hours do I work? Am I working too many?

8) What am I doing for my next vacation? When?

9) Do I know when to slow down and when to rest?

10) Who on my team is overworked?

11) What do I know about my team members' fitness levels?

9

12) In what ways do I cause stress for my team members?

13) What do I do to help my team members recover from intense efforts?

14) What do I do to help my team members pursue work/life balance?

Recognition: *The acknowledgement of achievement, service, merit, etc.*

If you were in a relationship with someone who continually demanded a lot from you, sapped your energy, expected your loyalty and otherwise ignored you, would you remain in the relationship?

For your sake, I hope not. There are more fish in the sea, right?

Let's say you just wrapped up a work project that required you to step up into a bigger leadership role, meet a tight deadline, meet a tight budget, bring home work night after night, and generally go above and beyond your normal job duties. If, afterward, you got no notable thanks, follow up, or other recognition from your manager, how would you feel? You may have hoped for something – perhaps a little gushing from your boss, if nothing else. In the absence of such, will you be inclined

10

to put in the same amount of effort next time? Will you want to remain in that relationship?

I suspect those would be tough questions. In fact, you might start to wonder how many other fish are out there.

> *"What every genuine philosopher (every genuine man, in fact) craves most is praise – although the philosophers generally call it 'recognition'!"*
> *- American philosopher and psychologist William James*

Basic Psychology

Employees, like the philosophers referenced above by William James, are people. And people need recognition. All people. As I briefly discussed in the previous chapter, humans all have questions, to one degree or another, about why we are here on Earth. We spend our lives searching and striving for meaning. And, so, the least we can do as fellow people is to acknowledge each other's existence, which is even more foundational than meaning.

> *"We have an innate propensity to get ourselves noticed, and noticed favorably, by our kind. No more fiendish punishment could be devised, were such a thing physically possible, than that one should be turned loose in society and remain absolutely unnoticed." - William James*

When work goes unnoticed or underappreciated, I believe it fuels our existential angst. I'm not sure we need constant praise, as I'll discuss more. But, at bare minimum, we need to be acknowledged. That is basic to the human condition.

Don't just take it from William James or me. Psychologist Abraham Maslow, whose famous "hierarchy of needs" is wide-

10

ly referenced in business circles, also indicated that recognition was a basic human need. He called it the need for "esteem."

Here's the good news for leaders: people don't just need recognition; they also respond to it. Basic psychology tells us that people change their behavior based on consequences. The psychologists call it "operant conditioning." But most of the rest of us call it "obvious." When you reinforce people's behavior, they are likely to continue it. When you "punish" people's behavior, to use the psychology term, they are likely to change it. And when you ignore people's behavior, they are likely to do less of that behavior and eventually stop it altogether.

I reference all of this to make the point that recognition is not a touchy-feely exercise, as some managers might believe. It's not simply a nice thing to do. And it's not all about fun and games. It's science. Yes, positive recognition does tend to make people feel good. But, more than that, it drives business. By fulfilling our team members' basic need for acknowledgement and esteem, and by providing feedback that either reinforces behavior or encourages new behavior, we ensure we get the most out of our greatest resource – people.

Benefits of Recognition

With more and better recognition practices, we can expect the following:

- Improved Performance
- Reduced Turnover
- Improved Team Culture

Improved Performance

Recognition drives team performance in many ways. First, it

reinforces positive contributions, which encourages those recognized to continue making those sorts of contributions or to strive for even more. Second, when it's visible, it's a powerful communication message that motivates other team members to make similarly positive contributions. Third, when we also recognize less-than-positive contributions and make course corrections, we avoid the perils of ongoing poor performance. Fourth, by reducing turnover, we avoid some of the productivity losses that generally come with transitions to new team members. And fifth, by creating an honest and positive culture, we keep morale high, sustain motivation and avoid some of the productivity dips that are experienced by other teams whose morale waxes and wanes more.

Reduced Turnover

This is pretty simple. People whose basic need for esteem is met tend to remain in their jobs longer. When people know their boss cares enough to provide feedback, they tend to stick around. Not only does this reduce turnover costs, but it also creates more institutional knowledge within your team, which can be valuable. In addition, it allows us to promote careers, not just jobs, and that helps with succession planning as well as recruiting. In short, while pay and benefits may attract talent, recognition stands the best chance of retaining it. That has been my experience.

Improved Team Culture

People who get regular, balanced feedback tend to trust their leaders more. And people whose positive contributions are recognized, rather than overlooked or taken for granted, generally have positive attitudes. The nice thing about trust is that it tolerates mistakes, which all of us are prone to making. The nice thing about positive attitudes is that they are contagious (i.e. team members may even start to recognize each other). Trust and positivity, together, help to create and maintain morale, or "esprit de corps," which keeps team members believing in our goals and objectives even when times get tough. Pride and loyalty abound in high-morale cultures.

Sometimes, public recognition also serves to educate others in our organization about the positive contributions our team members make. This, in turn, can generate positive feedback for our team, which improves morale further, and can pique the interest of talented others who may want to join our team.

Costs of Recognition

Recognition does not have to be expensive. It can range from fancy trips and award banquets for your elite performers to more affordable, everyday acts of letting people know, "Hey, you did a good job and really helped the organization." Given that variability, costs can include time needed to give recognition; time and cost of teaching leaders how to give recognition; time spent designing and implementing any formal recognition programs; cost of any rewards that accompany the recognition; and cost of introducing a formal recognition process.

For my money, day-to-day recognition presents the biggest opportunity. Obviously, it's more affordable. But it also can be more effective in reinforcing behavior since it's generally more frequent and personal than formal recognition programs.

> *"People often say that motivation doesn't last. Well, neither does bathing – that's why we recommend it daily."*
> *- motivation guru Zig Ziglar*

In many respects, recognition seems to be a no-brainer. And yet most business experts I've met or read say it is an underval-

10

ued and oft-neglected opportunity. But why? Some argue that a lot of leaders simply aren't comfortable giving feedback, particularly positive feedback. Others say it's simply an issue of ineffective leadership execution. Still others believe many leaders miss the point altogether. Have you ever heard: "Employees are lucky enough to have a job in this economy;" "Why should I recognize or thank them for doing their jobs?" or "We're running a business here. We don't have time for games."

Such comments ignore the science of recognition. They also ignore author Ron Willingham's wise business axiom of the *People Principle*, which says organizational efforts should focus on how to maximize the loyalty of customers and dedication of employees. As you'll see in the next section, recognition has a pretty clear impact on both of those sets of people.

The Statistics

Let's talk about evidence now – both for the clear opportunity that recognition represents for its recipients and for the clear return that leaders can expect on their recognition investments.

An outfit called Sirota Consulting did an amazingly thorough study of this topic from 1993 to 2003, interviewing 2.5 million employees in 237 private, public and nonprofit organizations in 89 countries. Sirota's surveys found that only 51 percent of workers were satisfied with the recognition they received for a job well done.

So what? Well, a 2005 Northwestern University study found a direct link between employee satisfaction and customer satisfaction, as well as between customer satisfaction and improved financial performance. In addition, a recent study by the Gallup Organization determined that employee recognition is one of the 12 key dimensions of great workplaces because of its impact on employee engagement. Gallup's research found that

10

the earnings per share (EPS) of companies in the top 25 percent for employee engagement exceeds competition by 28 percent, while the EPS of companies in the top 10 percent for employee engagement exceeds competition by a whopping 72 percent. Furthermore, companies in the top 25 percent for employee engagement surpassed lesser-engaged competitors during the big recession year of 2008, while the most engaged companies widened their lead on the competition, according to Derek Irvine, co-author with Eric Mosley of the book, *Winning with a Culture of Recognition.* EPS is not the only business outcome related to employee engagement. A 2007-2008 study by Towers Perrin (now Towers Watson) found that com-

panies with high engagement also outperform their low-engagement counterparts in terms of operating income and income growth rate.

Nationwide, almost a decade into the 2000s, employee engagement remained at its lowest level in 15 years, according to a Hewitt survey cited by Mosley and Irvine. So, again, the opportunity is clear: a lot of people feel underappreciated; recognizing them fuels engagement in the business; and engagement leads to happier customers and better business results.

In 2003, Gallup compiled results from several studies that collectively looked at 10,000 business units in 30 industries, and found support for much of what we've discussed in this chapter. Specifically, Gallup found that more and better recognition results in the following:

- Increased individual productivity in support of the

organization's mission and key performance indicators.
- Greater employee satisfaction and enjoyment of work - more time spent focusing on the job and less time complaining.
- Direct performance feedback for individuals and teams.
- Higher loyalty and satisfaction scores from customers.
- Enhanced teamwork between employees.
- Increased retention of quality employees.
- Better safety records and fewer accidents on the job.
- Lower absenteeism and stress.

Just consider turnover alone. According to the Bureau of Labor Statistics and Society of Human Resources Management, it costs anywhere from 33 percent to 150 percent of an employee's base salary to replace him or her. For a company of 1,000 employees with an average salary base of $50,000 and annual turnover of about 10 percent, that's a cost of $1.7 million to $7.5 million per year. Obviously, even a single percentage point improvement in turnover can save hundreds of thousands of dollars, if not millions. And, again, recognition is clearly related. In a 1997 study by McKinsey and Company, 65 percent of respondents cited not "feeling valued" or "insufficient recognition or reward" as a reason for leaving their previous employer.

Recognize What?

Yes, most things worthy of recognition are obvious: hard work, loyalty, dedication, dependability, and other positive personal qualities. We find it easiest to recognize those who set the example for other team members. We also like to recognize results. Project completions. Money saved. Sales generated. Efficiencies gained. Typically, however, we're worst at recognizing the most important thing – the specific behaviors that represent personal qualities and produce results.

10

Behaviors

Remember, the most powerful aspect of recognition is its reinforcing capability. But recognition that praises results or personal qualities without addressing specific behaviors may not be reinforcing at all. For example, if you say to an employee,

"Thank you for finishing that project under budget,"

the employee will know what he or she knew from the start – that you wanted the project completed within budget. However, you also could have said something like this:

"Thank you for negotiating a new rate with our vendor. I wasn't necessarily counting on that. But by proactively doing it, you were able to make up for the unanticipated cost overruns in IT even before we knew about them. Ultimately, it allowed you to complete the project under budget, and I want to thank you for that. And I specifically want to commend you for looking for savings even when you were not specifically asked to do so. That was a great way of supporting the company's strategy of reducing costs."

I hope you can see that the second alternative is more effective as reinforcement because it zeroes in on the specific behavior that led to the results. The employee is now more likely to proactively look for cost savings in the future.

Similarly, you could praise a personal quality, such as:

"Thanks for always being so dependable."

That has some reinforcing value. But, you could accomplish more by saying:

10

"I appreciate that you communicate with me so often when it comes to progress on your projects. I don't always like the updates, but I also never get surprises. I like being able to depend on you in that way."

The focus, regardless of what we're recognizing, should be on specific behaviors. At the same time, it's important to always connect those behaviors we recognize to the business results we expect, as well as to our organization's values, vision, mission, or goals. That's our chance to align the stars, so to speak, and infuse strategy into the organizational culture.

Effort v. Results

One thing in particular I would like to address is the reluctance some leaders have in recognizing effort even when the results fail to meet expectations. As I've discussed in previous chapters, all people fall short from time to time, so to deny recognition for valiant efforts is to deny reality and jeopardize one's own credibility as a leader, in my view. Of course, praising hard work does not require praising the results. So, when appropriate, go ahead and praise the effort (even noisily if warranted) and, at the same time, coach on the results. Examine why the effort did not match the results. Perhaps the effort was misguided in some way, or perhaps uncontrollable outside factors affected the results. Whatever the case, focus on the behavior and connect to the results, even when the results are subpar.

Positive v. Negative Behavior

Another thing I wanted to specifically address in this section is the need to recognize both positive and negative behavior. I have focused primarily on reinforcing positive behavior – those behaviors we want to see repeated. But I want to emphasize that it's also important to recognize behaviors that need to stop or change. As I mentioned earlier, psychologists refer to this type of recognition as "punishment." Of course, we generally prefer terms such as constructive feedback or coaching. Whatever you want to call it, it's valuable. The key is to keep our recognition balanced – in other words, recognize all kinds of behaviors.

I had an old Army sergeant – Sgt. Tiller – who was a real model for me as a leader because he always recognized outstanding performance but also never failed to recognize average or below average performance. He was one of those guys who once guarded the Tomb of the Unknown Soldier and, forever after, always looked, acted and performed like a soldier. He could be intimidating in appearance. But, in leadership personality, he was fair, honest and sincere. He seemed like someone who genuinely wanted us to excel – someone who genuinely cared about us. And we respected him as a result. To me, his respect was rooted in his very balanced recognition practices. He built our esteem, and we appreciated that. But he also had the courage and cared enough to be honest with us when we needed to change. Either way, he was positive, providing

Tomb of the Unknown Soldier

help, rather than punishment. At least that's how we viewed it. I've thought a lot about how he was able to strike such a delicately effective balance. My conclusion, however, is embarrass-

10

ingly simple. Part of it is the positive tone. Beyond that, I think he just spent a little more time on praise than criticism and, by doing so, he kept us open to his coaching.

In that regard, Sgt. Tiller's approach supports Gallup research that says managers who focus on employee strengths have 61 percent engaged employees and just 1 percent actively disengaged. Meanwhile, managers who focus on weaknesses have 45 percent-engaged employees and 22 percent actively disengaged. Worse yet, according to the research, are managers who ignore their employees; they have only 2 percent engaged employees and 40 percent actively disengaged.

This brings up the question of whether gratitude can be overdone. Indeed, some managers believe thanks and praise should be saved for special occasions. I disagree. My experience is that sincere thanks and praise are always received sincerely, regardless of frequency. It's just a matter of remaining sincere. Like Gallup and Sgt. Tiller, I've also found that, in the long run, criticism doesn't work as well as encouragement, positivity, and inspiration. So, while balance is critical, if our recognition ever leans one way or the other, it ought to be toward praise.

Types of Recognition
Informal, day-to-day recognition

Work is unrelenting. We go to work, go home, get up the next day and go to work again. Day after day. Week after week. Year after year. Ideally, we enjoy and are fulfilled by the work. But, either way, given the rigor, it's a challenge to stay motivated, whether you're an executive or a factory worker. That's why recognition is so important as an everyday practice – it helps to sustain motivation.

When I say everyday practice, I don't necessarily mean that we need to recognize every single team member every day. For most of us, that's not possible. What I do mean is that recognition should become a routine and natural part of your leadership approach – a philosophy, you might say, that is evident in the little things you do each day.

Greet people by name. Shake people's hands and say thanks for a job well done. Praise and compliment them verbally. Write personalized notes from time to time. Small tokens of appreciation are important.

Bob Nelson, in his book *1001 Ways to Reward Employees*, suggests, "Some of the best forms of recognition (personal or written praise, public recognition, positive voicemail or e-mail messages, etc.) require very little time to do."

Make sure you also take advantage of regular 1:1 assessments with your team members – not just annual appraisals, but even weekly, monthly or quarterly check-ins. Don't take these meetings lightly or use them simply to get updates on projects. Provide balanced feedback and accentuate the positive. These are strategic recognition opportunities.

The same is true for team meetings, whether virtual or in person. Take opportunities in these meetings to publicly recognize the work of your team and individual members. Make it one of your priorities for all such meetings.

Another idea for informal recognition is to establish a "kudos" board or "wall of fame." Pick a specific area in the workplace where you can post positive notes about your team members. They might be e-mails you receive from customers or others in the organization. Or, they could be original, personalized notes

10

you choose to write for public display. They also could be notes that team members write to recognize each other. Kudos boards can be powerful tools in building a recognition culture.

Yet another informal recognition strategy involves work assignments. Look for opportunities to give your team members new challenging assignments or even new jobs that recognize their achievements in current roles.

You probably have some of your own ideas for informal, day-to-day recognition, too. Go with those. If recognition is to be perceived as genuine, it must actually be genuine, so make sure to recognize using your own personal style.

And don't be afraid to ask your team members for recognition ideas. Doing so is an act of recognition itself. Just be careful of giving away your responsibilities. It's great if others get involved in recognizing each other, but that must be in addition to your involvement, not instead. People want recognition from their boss, first and foremost.

Formal recognition programs

While informal, day-to-day recognition may be inexpensive and easy to start right away, formal recognition programs can be even more effective in helping to achieve specific goals. The downside is that they are more expensive and often require the involvement of others (such as HR).

The Schwan Food Company, where I worked, had a fairly typical recognition program for its home delivery sales team. If salespeople met certain criteria during specified sales periods, they earned awards points that could be redeemed for catalog prizes. We also had specific short-term contests, such as our seafood sales contest, which provided winners with bonus prizes, such as an all-expenses-paid cruise. Most notably, we had club levels based on annual sales goals. The organization's

10

top salespeople earned entry into the exclusive Chairman's Club, which entitled them to public recognition at an annual banquet, a gold watch and other prizes, and the respect of their peers.

It was an expensive program, requiring a significant investment of time and money. Most of the time, it appeared to be a key driver of business results, but not always. We constantly monitored the return on our investment and tweaked the program to improve or maintain a good return. For example, back in the company's heyday, our formal recognition programs clearly boosted morale and helped to create a positive work environment. We had a unique business model that fit with the times, and we were growing consistently year over year. As a result, the recognition targets were attainable for anyone willing to put in the work. However, when the company began to mature and growth slowed, the recognition targets became more unattainable to the masses. Many salespeople began to ignore and even resent the contests and targets. Over time, we ended up having to change everything – the prizes, targets, contest frequency, etc. – to make sure we were contributing to morale instead of sapping it and producing an investment return rather than a loss.

That is the key with formal recognition programs – because of their expense, they must be equally powerful for both the organization and the employee. They need a specific focus and goal, and require a cost-benefit analysis, which isn't always easy. For example, if you're considering a safety recognition program that costs $500, you need to figure out a way to es-

10

timate the potential long-term savings from that investment. In designing your programs, I recommend developing specific criteria, a time frame and benchmarks for measuring progress. Promote the program with a kickoff event and progress reports. And make sure your awards are meaningful enough to motivate employees and encourage their participation; with formal recognition programs, the size or amount of the benefit can matter.

Also avoid designing a process in which leaders mysteriously "select" the people to receive recognition. Charges of "favoritism" will cause a program to backfire quickly. The last thing you want to overhear is, "Oh, I guess it's your turn to get recognized this month." Instead, use clear, simple and specific criteria so that everyone understands enough to compete and so that anyone who performs at the established standard earns the recognition.

Recognition Do's

- **Be specific.** When providing recognition, describe the particular situation and task that a team member faced, the action he or she took, and the result. Make it easy for the team member to see exactly what you are reinforcing.

- **Be balanced.** Lean toward positive feedback, but also make sure to give critical feedback. And when you do, be just as specific. Describe the situation and task faced, the action taken, the result – only this time, make sure to also discuss alternative actions that could be taken next time, and the alternative results one could expect.
- **Be timely.** Once again, the science of psychology helps us here. It says that the more immediately a consequence is

10

ZERO TO SOMETHING LEADERSHIP

felt, the more effectively that consequence will influence future behavior. In other words, don't save your praise and criticism for formal reviews or events. And don't shy away from spontaneity. Recognize behavior as soon as you become aware of it; if you do so, the praise will be more reinforcing and the criticism will be more likely to prompt change.

- **Be sincere.** This often trumps tangible value in our team members' eyes. So, truly think about and mean what you say. Express appreciation in your own way. Be creative. Don't go through the motions. People can spot fakeness a mile away.

- **Be consistent.** Don't go through spells of plentiful and minimal recognition. And avoid recognizing a certain type of behavior one time and then ignoring it the next. Our team members get confused when we are too random. And, sure enough, psychology tells us that consistent reinforcing leads to faster learning.

- **Be fair.** It's quite natural for leaders to develop favorite employees – people with whom you share common interests, people who have earned a great deal of your respect or trust, etc. So, don't feel bad if you have favorites. Just keep in mind that, even if you may have favorites, it's important not to display favoritism. Watch yourself so that you do not overly target a specific employee or group of employees with your recognition. Don't become blinded by your favorites at the expense of others. Jealousy can quickly turn to a sense of injustice, which will erode your leadership legitimacy as sure as anything. So, be fair and always remain an equal-opportunity recognizer.

- **Individualize.** Being fair does not mean giving everyone the same type of recognition. Some team members may respond well to a widely circulated newsletter recognizing their exploits. Others may prefer extra time and attention from the boss. Similarly, some may respond better to earning extra money or prizes while others may prefer earning the removal of obstacles, hassles and frustrations. Know your team members, and know what is meaningful to them. Apply a personal touch.

- Generally speaking, **praise in public and be critical in private**. This is a matter of respect, and, from a practical standpoint, it maximizes the impact of your feed-back by minimizing defensiveness and resentment. But keep in mind, when it comes to praise, some people are not always comfortable receiving it publicly. So, as I mentioned above, learn what your team members like and individualize.

- **Use variety.** Once again, the psychologists help by confirming the obvious: people will grow tired of the same old recognition, and it will eventually influence their behavior less and less. Team members may even come to see the recognition or reward as an entitlement. At the same time, the psychologists say, if a perk can be enjoyed and then expire, people will be motivated to get it back. Both of these bits of science cry for variety. So, mix it up a little.

10

- **Share your feelings.** When providing recognition, explain how someone's behavior made you feel. It's powerfully reinforcing to learn that your boss felt pride, respect or happiness because of what you did. It also can be a powerful motivator for change to learn that your boss was disappointed. So, as a leader, don't just stick to the facts. Share how you're feeling.

- **Recognize frequently** – Don't be stingy with gratitude. Recognize as often as possible, just so long as you remain sincere.

- **Link recognition to organizational priorities.** Formal recognition programs must absolutely and directly support the organization's values, vision, mission and goals. But it's also critical to link informal day-to-day recognition to those priorities. When recognizing people, point out how their behavior supports or contradicts company priorities. Don't expect the organization's culture to magically spring from priorities set to paper. Unless those leadership statements are reinforced daily with various forms of recognition, they will simply gather dust. This is what makes recognition strategic.

Recognition Don'ts

- **Don't apply a price tag to everything.** In other words, don't make it too difficult to earn your praise or attention, and recognize good behaviors even when the results fall short or have yet to be realized. Imagine you

10

are an offensive line coach in football. Would you only praise a good block when it leads to a touchdown? Would you fail to criticize a bad block even when a touchdown was scored? In both cases, I hope not.

- **Don't promote cutthroat competitiveness.** Instead, promote cooperation and success for everyone. This can be tricky in naturally competitive environments such as sales. But, to the degree possible, try not to pit your team members against each other. You want them to stand out by propping themselves up, not tearing each other down. So, speak to that. And provide critical feedback to those who pursue success and recognition at the expense or exclusion of the team.

- **Don't turn the task of recognition over to HR.** Formal rewards programs may necessarily require HR partnership, but avoid putting HR in charge and washing your hands of this aspect of your business. Doing so will make your programs meaningless, like a birthday card with a stamped signature. Remember that recognition and rewards are most effective coming from an employee's boss.

Next Steps

If recognition is an area of leadership you choose to improve, I suggest starting discreetly, without even telling your team members. Start with the informal, day-to-day recognition that is inexpensive, effective and immediately achievable.

The primary change will be in your mindset. To begin, you will need to start identifying and realizing more opportunities to praise people. Then, you'll need to experiment with methods of delivering your praise in a way that effectively reinforces the behavior and links it to the organization's priorities. You may also need to experiment with ways of offering critical feedback. In both cases, you will need to find out what feels comfortable and fits your personality.

It may sound corny, but I have found that keeping a journal is a good way of instituting changes such as these. Keep it on your desk for a few weeks or longer. Take a couple minutes each day to jot down a few notes about the recognition opportunities you saw, what you did, how it was received, and how it felt to you. In addition, you might reflect on what this skill means to your leadership, how it relates to your team's potential for success, and what goals you might have for the next day.

Journaling is just one way to make your new recognition mindset stick, so that it becomes part of who you are as a leader. Another suggestion would be to discuss your efforts with your boss. Make it part of your own development plan. Whichever way you want to approach it, developing recognition as a core strength will require commitment and practice.

The next thing I suggest, beyond the daily recognition efforts, is to make recognition a more purposeful part of your existing 1:1 meetings with team members, to include weekly and monthly check-ins as well as quarterly and annual reviews. You don't necessarily need to create new meetings. Just make a conscious effort to provide more recognition – both praise and critical feedback – in the meetings you're already having.

As your skill becomes more advanced, you also may want to consider more formal recognition programs as well. In that case, I suggest involving your boss and HR in considering various ideas and conducting thorough cost-benefit analyses.

10

Reflections

Recognition is another win-win, providing both leaders and our teams with what we need from work. We meet their basic need for acknowledgement and esteem, which conditions them to be exactly what we need – successful, happy, productive and positive. In addition, recognition provides us with more opportunities to align the stars by connecting individual behavior to organizational vision, mission and goals.

Lest we forget, it also feels good – not just to receive recognition, but to give it. And that remains important. At times, we're all a little anxious about downsizing, restructuring and the world's uncertain economic climate. So, cultivating an attitude of gratitude is something from which we all can benefit.

As you think more about this cornerstone to great leadership, consider these reflective questions:

1) Why is recognition important to your leadership effectiveness?

2) Are you a leader known for recognizing your team members?

3) What sort of things do you recognize most? Least?

4) Do you recognize team members who demonstrate the R's of leadership, even if they are individual contributors? For example …

   a. Do you recognize people who use resources efficiently?

   b. Do you recognize people who follow the rules?

   c. Do you recognize people who foster supportive relationships?

   d. Do you recognize people who are realistic, respectful to others, responsible, and relentless?

    e. Do you recognize those who take risks?

    f. Do you recognize people who make recovery a priority and avoid criticizing people for it?

    g. Do you recognize those people who do a good job of recognizing others?

    h. Do you recognize those who take the time to reflect positively on past, current, and future actions?

5) What are some examples of you adhering to the guideline of praising in public and offering critical feedback in private?

6) How would you describe your style of recognition?

7) What about your recognition efforts is lacking?

8) Are you least comfortable providing praise or criticism?

9) Is your praise usually specific enough to be effective reinforcement? How could it be more specific?

10) In what ways do you link recognition to both business results and organizational priorities?

11) Have you ever been accused of favoritism? How could that have been avoided?

12) What is your plan for improving your day-to-day recognition efforts? What ideas do you have for formal recognition programs?

10

Reflection: *The deliberate act of rationally contemplating and carefully considering one's own thinking.*

As you near the end of this book, you may be anticipating a feeling of satisfaction and accomplishment – the fulfillment of finishing something you started.

But do you also sense the danger?

Yes, there's an inherent risk in finally taking in that last word. You are exposing yourself to the hazard of forgetting what you learned, or, perhaps, not applying what you learned. In either case, you risk having wasted your time.

No doubt you have attended many classes in your life. Conquered many books. Experienced many things. And, still, I wonder if this scenario sounds familiar: "Take the test. Pass it. Wonder some time later why you can no longer remember anything you learned."

Of all the things we learn in life, very little sticks. There's an old song, popularized by both Bob Dylan and Johnny Cash, entitled, "I Forgot More Than You'll Ever Know." Indeed, most of us have forgotten more than we'll ever know at any one time.

So, what sticks? What earns the privilege of residing in our memory banks and influencing our lives? And what gets thrown on the trash heap of our personal history?

In the education community, many argue that we retain those things we reflect upon most critically. When something challenges or confuses us, or presents conflict, we tend to reflect on it more critically. When we learn something and then are faced with integrating it into our own lives and experiences, we tend to reflect more critically. When we question our own understanding of something, and compare it to other understandings, we are critically reflecting and, as a result, learning in a way more likely to stick. Sometimes, critical reflection is needed to even identify what was learned. For example, when we take the time to analyze our own actions and outcomes, we figure out what we learned. At that point, of course, we're able to reflect even more.

Exposure is one thing. True learning is another. We can learn some bit of information, or even how to do something new. But, as your own experience surely can attest, if you don't apply it or in some way critically reflect upon it, you will quickly forget what you learned. "Use it or lose it" is a fitting axiom. But even that can oversimplify or mislead, since "use it" implies an action, when the real value is in the thinking behind our actions.

Have you ever revisited something rather mundane and, for some reason, remembered precisely where and when you

11

learned about it? For example, I recall where, when, and with whom I learned that peanut butter and honey go well together, particularly on English muffins. I also remember all the details surrounding the day when I learned that the word "notorious" means "infamous," not "famous." At the same time, I'm sure I learned some things last week that I have already lost. So, what is it? Why does some stuff stick and other stuff slide?

It's not as if I use the word "notorious" very often, after all. The reason I remember its meaning to this day is because I was so astounded that my high school English teacher docked points for my misusing it in a paper. I thought I had seen that word a million times and was confused. I challenged the teach-

er on it and eventually was proven wrong, discovering along the way that "notorious" is often misused. I looked up the definition, found examples of its misuse, found some commentary on its frequent misuse, and ate crow with my teacher. In short, I reflected upon it – much more critically than if "notorious" had simply been one of 20 vocabulary words I had to memorize.

For decades, educators have plotted how best to help students think in these ways. They know the research, which confirms its overwhelmingly positive impact on learning, retention and application. The whole concept of "reflective thinking" was introduced in a 1910 work by John Dewey entitled "How We Think." He wrote it mainly for teachers, and the premise was basically this: reflection improves learning. In 1933, he went further by defining reflective thinking in more detail: "Active,

11

persistent and careful consideration of any belief or supposed form of knowledge in the light of the grounds that support it and the further conclusion to which it tends."

Some academics consider "critical thinking" to be a synonymous term, but I prefer "reflective thinking" because I think it more accurately describes the act of contemplating one's *own* thinking.

How does this relate to leadership in the business world and elsewhere? Well, just as with educators, it's all about learning. Leaders, in order to be effective, need to constantly and continuously learn. We also need to create environments where our followers learn. If we don't, we'll be left in the dust of leaders and teams who are better able to learn, grow and adapt.

When many people think of learning, they generally think of training – and not just training, but, specifically, training events such as classes, seminars, online courses, etc. I'm a passionate supporter of learning in many forms, but I think we too often overlook the learning that can occur from reflective thinking, which is typically less expensive and more powerful than training events.

A Mindset, A Way to Check In, and A Way to Look Back

The Reflective Mindset: Humility, Contemplation and Growth

Reflective thinking, first, is a mindset. It's a commitment to humility – to challenging one's own thoughts and actions. It's a commitment to occasionally taking two steps back to look at yourself, your team, your company and your projects as if you are not an actor in the play but an objective observer. Leaders with this mindset spend quiet, contemplative time – away from the day-to-day race, perhaps coinciding with "Recovery" – taking stock of various situations and their own leadership.

11

They also find confidantes who will challenge their thinking and provide feedback on their leadership experiences. Reflective thinkers seek others' opinions more generally, too. They're committed to getting it right, not being right. As you might suspect, leaders with this mindset also tend to display a commitment to individual development – to developing their skills and not surviving solely on talent.

The best leaders carry this mindset with them always. Ironically, they think reflectively without even thinking about it. But getting to that point takes practice. Even if you're naturally in-clined to reflect, it can be a challenge to direct your reflections in a purpose-ful way. It's one thing to let your mind wander or race from one thing to another; it's another to reflect on specific aspects of your leadership, team, projects or goals with the intent of drawing conclu-sions. It's the deliberate act of reflecting that pro-vides specific new learn-ing and synthesizes old learning into new contexts.

Reflective Leaders (clockwise): President Abraham Lincoln, President Dwight Eisenhower, Martin Luther King Jr., & Gen. Colin Powell

Reflective Gut Checks: A Way to Check In

Reflective thinking also is, more specifically, a way of perform-ing gut checks before major implementations or decisions. Dan-iel Patrick Forrester, in his book *Consider: Harnessing the Power of Reflective Thinking*, described the reflective gut check by quoting University of California professor Dr. Robert Bea, who said: "Stop, think and don't do something stupid." That sums it up pretty well. As soon as you've got a plan in place or are ready to make a decision, take the time to check all your assumptions, review your thinking, and assess what you've learned in getting to that point. Don't just pull the trigger.

Now, I agree there is a danger of developing analysis paralysis. Acting without thinking, and thinking without action, are both deadly. The challenge, of course, is finding the right balance. My belief, however, is that today's business climate demands more reflection than ever. Modern society is complex. Information becomes available and changes rapidly. As a result, we need to constantly rethink, change directions and switch strategies. Technology allows us to give partial attention to many things but, in doing so, discourages us from giving our full attention to anything. We spend less and less time considering decisions before making them. These days, problem solving is often nothing more than a series of e-mails with an occasional face-to-face meeting sprinkled in. We are tethered to our smart phones and find ourselves constantly bombarded with more "stuff." Time for reflection rarely presents itself. And yet, Forrester, in his book, provides compelling evidence supporting the notion that the best decisions, insights, ideas and outcomes result when we take sufficient time to think and reflect.

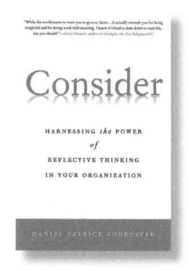

That, I feel, is why it's so important to make the time for reflection. Mindful of the risks of over-analysis, though, I've come to understand that reflective gut checks do not need to involve major investments of time or money. Quiet, contemplative time may be enough. Conversations with objective peers, bosses or confidantes may be most appropriate. Or, a meeting with the project team might be needed so that you can ask challenging questions. In any case, remember that the point of a reflective gut check is to prevent you from doing "something stupid." It may lead you to changing an entire project or approach, tweaking some aspect of what you're doing, or going full steam ahead with more confidence – all of which are valuable when warranted. In other words, reflective gut checks are worth it, whether they reinforce what you're doing or lead to changes. You and your team will learn a lot by constantly challenging your own thinking and being open to proverbial "outside the box" alternatives. You may learn, as I have occasionally, that even when you're solving problems the right way, you may not be solving the right problems. In fact, that's one very important conclusion that can only be reached via reflective thinking.

Reflective Reviews: A Way to Look Back

While gut checks can be performed multiple times and at any point during the course of a project or decision-making process, reflective thinking is perhaps most associated with looking back at the conclusion of such efforts.

> *"Reflective thinking turns experience into insight."*
> *– John Maxwell*

Reviewing projects at the end is something many leaders "know" to do. But, too often, it's done as a routine, with little passion and even less commitment to applying anything learned to future projects. This is often the fault of the leader, whose attention span can be even more limited than the typical

11

employee and who may not even participate in such post-project reviews. In my opinion, these reviews need to be led by the leader (imagine that) and should result in expectations for future efforts – expectations for which the leader is ultimately responsible and that often mean more to the leader's future success than to any individual's.

Reflective thinking boils down to asking questions, and that's exactly what happens in a reflective review. What the heck just happened? Why did it happen? Did we accomplish what we wanted to? What did we learn? What surprised us? What would we do differently? Did we have the R's squared away (i.e. did we have clear rules, respectful relationships, etc.)? Was our effort worth it? Did we solve the right problem? Did we act with positive intent at all times (in other words, were our motives sincere, transparent, and noble)? Did we do the best we could, with limited personal agendas? What about it was most or least fulfilling, and what does that say about our values? Which of our assumptions were right, and which were wrong? What should we do to be better next time?

Some like to narrow it all down to this simple framework – What? So what? Now what? Even more leaders are fond of the good old Start-Stop-Continue exercise, in which you ask yourself or the team: What should be started? What should be stopped? And what should be continued? In the Army, we called them "after-action" reviews.

However you choose to approach reflective reviews, make them robust. Don't make them routine or let them remain surface level. Dig deep into some of the questions and issues. Make the time you spend meaningful. Reflective thinking is a "pause for the cause" – a coming to terms and coming to peace with what happened. If integrated into project plans and given the serious attention they deserve, reflective reviews will develop

11

your team much more than many other training and development strategies.

One Prerequisite

While reflective thinking leads to learning, neither is possible without one prerequisite: a genuinely open mind. We leaders must be willing to hear feedback from confidantes. Willing to listen to our own conscience. Willing to hear honest assessments from our followers during gut checks and post-project reviews. Willing to be imperfect or even wrong. Willing to change our minds or change directions. Willing to be human.

We need to allow others to be human as well. We must encourage "thinking out loud" when appropriate and make sure there are no negative consequences to healthy dissent and debate. If our reflective thinking efforts are a charade, our followers will sense it, and such efforts will quickly become a waste of everyone's time.

One Distinction

At this point, you might be wondering how reflective thinking relates to the chapter on Reality and the notion of conducting informal and formal reality checks. Let me clarify. Reality checks are, in fact, a form of reflective thinking – a type of reflective gut check. If you made that connection, you are, in fact, thinking reflectively. If you did not, don't worry – I didn't either initially. Reality checks are all about making sure we don't kid ourselves – that we're not delusional or blinded by our own hopes or leadership bubble – that we're open to the truth, as I mentioned above. Reflective thinking is about that and more. It's about making sure we reflect, not just on what is real, but on what we are doing, what we've done, where we are, where we're going, etc. We obviously can reflect on any number of

11

things. If, in doing so, we make sure to always "keep it real," we'll achieve the learning we desire.

Next Steps

I recommend first dedicating some time to reflect on your own leadership and situation. In your mind, remove yourself from the day-to-day tasks and demands, and reflectively think about what is going well and what isn't going so well. Think about the big picture of your impact. Take some time to reflective-

ly think about people who have had an impact on your leadership style and why they impacted you so. Consider both those who taught you what to do and those who taught you what not to do, and think about why you make such distinctions. Look at your organization's leadership. Do the characteristics of the senior leaders transcend their areas of responsibility? Do yours? How would you describe their leadership style? How would you describe yours? What would those you lead say if they read or heard your description? Would they agree or disagree? Which R's of Leadership are your strengths? Which are weaknesses? Is your team, department or division heading in the direction you're supposed to be leading it? What could the concept of "Zero to Something" mean to you and your team?

> *"I'm Gonna Make A Change, For Once In My Life, It's Gonna Feel Real Good, Gonna Make A Difference, Gonna Make It Right"* - Michael Jackson, *from the very reflective song "Man in the Mirror"*

Consider capturing your reflections in a journal and discussing them with at least one confidante or mentor. From there, determine what you can change and what you can't change, and then take action. Are you going to attend training? Are you going to form a peer support group? Are you going to enlist the services of a leadership coach? Mentors?

As you dedicate time to these reflections, note when and where you feel most engaged in such thoughts. Is it while taking a walk; going on a long, slow run; listening to music at home; sitting in a coffee shop; or staying late at the office, perhaps? Determine where and when you do your best reflective thinking.

Next, I recommend picking a time when you feel particularly caught up in the heat of a leadership challenge – when things are moving fast, uncertainty is high, and you are a bit overwhelmed. Then, I want you to do the unthinkable – make time to step away for a short while, and go back to that place where you do your best reflective thinking. Engage a confidante or remain in solitude. Either way, remove yourself both physically and mentally from the situation, and do your best to review it from an objective, third-party perspective. See what sort of clarity it provides, and roll with any fresh perspectives you develop.

Following these first deliberate "pauses for the cause," I recommend trying a reflective gut-check with whatever team is involved in your current challenge. No doubt, you have had similar meetings, but focus this time on asking more reflective questions, such as: Have we learned anything yet that would indicate another direction might be better? What should we do differently? Do we have clear roles, rules and responsibilities? Respectful relationships? Are we solving the right problem? Is it worth it?

Focus on not only asking more reflective questions but on emphasizing and demonstrating your willingness to hear honest answers – reality. Even if you ultimately determine you're on the best course, you will have the benefit of proceeding with more confidence and, presumably, an even more engaged team.

After you have done your initial reflection journal, experimented with taking a "pause for the cause" in the midst of a specific business challenge, and held your first reflective gut-check meeting, I recommend planning your first reflective post-project review. Even if you've held such reviews in the past, focus this time on engaging your team more than ever with thoughtful, reflective questions. Plan the questions ahead of time. Send them out in advance so people have time to think prior to the meeting. Encourage candor and vulnerability. Be candid and vulnerable yourself. Assume responsibility for making sure identified learnings are integrated into the next project.

Most importantly, don't expect to do all these things at once. A big aspect of reflection is taking the time to breathe. Overwhelming yourself with it would defeat the purpose. As always, the "Zero to Something" philosophy applies. Make some progress. And then make some more. Continuous improvement is the key – to both this book and this chapter.

Reflections

As you may have noticed, I've tried to encourage reflection throughout this book. At the end of each chapter, I've included reflective questions intended to help you integrate what you have read into your own life, career and experiences. They're also intended to challenge you about

11

your own current skill levels. I guess you could call them reflective gut checks. I hope that, along the way, you also have enhanced the reflective mindset that got you to pick up this book in the first place. Finally, I hope that you will take  time immediately after finishing this book to do a reflective look back at the book in its entirety. I encourage you to reflect on the "Zero to Something" philosophy, the R's of Leadership, what you learned, how that relates to your current leadership situation and ultimate goals, what you want to apply, etc.

Before you get to the overall reflective review, however, here are some reflective questions to consider for this chapter's gut check:

1) What are some specific "a-ha" moments from your life – times when you specifically remember learning something that stuck?

2) In your own experience, why does certain information stick while other information is forgotten?

3) What are some things that didn't stick? (It's OK to be general; I know you can't remember the specifics!)

4) What does critical thinking, or reflective thinking, mean to you, in your own words?

5) When, from whom, and under what circumstances, do you seek feedback from others?

6) When have you had the courage and humility to change your mind, change course or admit you were wrong?

7) For you, has "being right" ever gotten in the way of "getting it right?"

8) While technology allows you to act and react more quickly than ever, in what ways do you make the time to consider decisions reflectively before making them?

9) Why is it important to take "a pause for the cause" even in the heat of battle?

10) In what ways do you teach your team members how to reflect on the past, current and future?

11) If you have previously led or participated in something resembling a reflective gut check or reflective review, what, if anything, was lacking?

12) What sort of current strategies do you have for taking two steps back and reflectively thinking about what has been done, what is being done, and what needs to be done in the future?

13) To what degree do you and your team members "keep it real" when reflecting on current or past efforts?

14) If you had to pick which side you erred on — action or analysis — which would it be and why?

15) What reflecting have you done on the individual R's of Leadership? How would continuous reflection help? And what would continuous reflection look like?

11

Conclusion

Congratulations! If you are reading this, you made it to the end of the book and have demonstrated a commitment to your leadership craft. You care, and that alone indicates great potential. Alternatively, you may be reading this because you skipped to the end or decided to start here. In that case, I am flattered you found the suspense just too much to bear! Either way, I'm happy you are inside the pages and want to commend you for not simply relying on your leadership instincts. We all have a lot to learn from each other.

By reading books such as this, finding and utilizing mentors, talking to our peers, and otherwise reaching out to strive for more, we support a lot beyond our own careers. We also help the people we lead, their families, our family, our organization, and, indirectly, all of the people touched by the organization, including customers. That's the reality of leadership – it has far-reaching, exponential impacts, for better or worse. In other words, we leaders bear great responsibility. While we can't take ourselves too seriously, we do have to take the role seriously, and that begins with always making the effort to improve. So, again, congratulations on the investment you have made in reading this book.

Now What?

Start Writing Your Own Book

One of the reasons I wrote this book was to provide others with an example of one person's attempt – mine – to synthesize all that I have learned about leadership over the years. As I mentioned in the Introduction chapter, the world is replete with leadership books. I've read many of them, and you'll see a new set of market entries every time you walk through the airport. Many cover the same ground. Many are almost offensive in their attempt to simplify or provide quick fixes. Yet, all have something to offer. The danger is in becoming either overwhelmed or cynical. My suggestion is to read all you can, but take what you want and leave the rest. Start your own leadership journal and think of it as notes for the book you will eventually write. Document what you learn from books, experiences, peers, bosses, etc. Writing, as we discussed in the last chapter, will help

you reflect on what you learned. Over time – as you learn, write and reflect more – patterns and themes will develop. You will naturally begin to synthesize your knowledge and will develop your own mental model for leadership – something that works for you. Do yourself a favor and abandon all hopes for a secret leadership panacea. Instead, pursue the very concept of this book – steady, meaningful progress. Allow your leadership to develop from zero (your current baseline) to something. Then reset the dial to zero and once again move from zero to something. Keep moving forward. Eventually you'll look back and realize that your consistent gains have added up to big growth. At that time, you can turn your journal into your own book.

First, though, start the journal. Open a new Microsoft Word® document, or use whatever word processor you prefer, and start ruminating about this book. Write about the things that connected with you most and least. Reflect on how the book relates to your strengths, opportunities and desires for growth. Write about what you plan to implement and how. Don't worry about writing perfectly (obviously, I never do!). Don't spend too much time or be too thorough. It doesn't need to be in book form yet. Spend as much time as you're willing or able to invest. Just make sure to write something. Start the process. Zero to something.

Try Stuff

In addition to starting your journal (or continuing it if you started while reading the previous chapters), I recommend that you start developing the habit of "trying stuff." If you are to reach any conclusions about leadership philosophies and techniques, you need to test-drive them and see what works for you.

While I have readily acknowledged the many debts I owe to other authors and leaders, this book is much more than a summary of existing literature. I've been using this model and constantly refining it for many years. It is more practical than philosophical, and that's because, for me, it is tried and true. As I learned more, I experimented more. Some of it stuck. Some of it didn't. Some of it helped. Some of it didn't. But I didn't know until I tried. I suppose that is an obvious notion. But, as I've mentioned before, we often overlook the obvious. So, make a conscious decision to implement what you learn. Give stuff a try, and then decide what to take and what to leave. Start by trying the concepts in this book, and start right now.

Prioritize Your Leadership SOPs

In these final pages, I have provided a couple of blank priority assessment forms, which are also available on my Web site - _zerotosomething.com_. Make copies of the form if you wish. It's a simple way of assessing your own skills and your team's needs so that you can quickly determine your priorities.

In the "Self Assessment" column, rank the R's, from 1 to 11, in terms of your current skills. For example, if your skills are least developed in the area of Results, rank that as 1, and if your skills are strongest in the area of Recovery, rank that as 11.

In the "Team Need" column, rank the R's, from 1 to 11, in terms of your team's current needs. For example, if your team would benefit most from a focus on appropriate Risk-Taking (i.e. that is the team's biggest need), rank that as 1. And if the team would benefit least from a focus on Respectful Relationships, perhaps because that is already a towering team strength, then rank that as 11.

As you do these two rankings for the first time, I suggest you look back at each chapter, particularly the reflections and questions at the end, to refresh your memory. Once you are comfortable with your rankings, add the two for each R and write the totals into the "Total" column.

Next, note that the lower totals represent your highest development priorities and the higher totals represent your lowest development priorities. In other words, your highest development priorities are the R's in which you are weakest and your team's needs are greatest. The R with the lowest total should be Priority #1 (in terms of your development), and the R with the highest total should be Priority #11. In the last column, write the priority for each R, from 1 to 11.

Your own development priorities (column #1) will not necessarily be your immediate action priorities. Indeed, if you have

	SELF ASSESSMENT (1=least developed; 11=most developed)	TEAM NEED (1=biggest need; 11=smallest need)	TOTAL (Add self-assessment and team need ranks)	DEVELOPMENT PRIORITY (1=R with lowest TOTAL; 11=R with highest TOTAL)
Results				
Reality				
Resources				
Rules				
Roles & Responsibilities				
Respectful Relationships				
Risk Taking				
Relentless Resolve				
Recovery				
Recognition				
Reflective Thinking				

Priority Assessment Form

a new team with a great need in one of your areas of strength, you should act immediately, using this book to supplement what you already know and do in that area. That's an opportunity to move quickly from zero to something. Take it!

The last-column priorities, rather, represent where you want to concentrate your *development* efforts. Pick the top two or three priorities for starters. Go back and review those chapters. Spend time thoroughly answering the reflective questions at the end of each chapter. Perhaps write your answers in your leadership journal. Develop some ideas for ways to implement improvements. Talk to your boss and peers about your ideas. And then give them a whirl. If one thing doesn't work, reflect with others on why it didn't. Revise and try again, or try something altogether different. Be wary of doing or expecting too much too quickly. Focus on our philosophy – zero to something. [ex.2]

Again, let me emphasize that there is no magic formula for where to focus your energy. I constructed the priority assessment as I did because our team's needs tend to reflect our own leadership deficiencies. In that way, combining the two rankings to determine our priorities makes sense. But, in some cases, particularly when you inherit a new team, your team's needs may have no relation to your own strengths and weaknesses. In that case, you may want to prioritize strictly according to team need, utilizing strengths and developing weaknesses as applicable. In any case, assess yourself and your team honestly, and use your best judgment in prioritizing.

Remember, too, that you can pull out this book and these forms at any time in the future. It's good to reassess from time to time. While you may become skilled at developing and fostering Respectful Relationships, for example, your team's relationships – with you, each other or possibly others outside the team – could still go south at any time. It's nearly impossible to keep everything humming at all times. And sometimes, as leaders, we get distracted.

I like to assess thoroughly whenever I take over a new team, by observing and in some cases, interviewing team members.

	SELF ASSESSMENT (1=least developed; 11=most developed)	TEAM NEED (1=biggest need; 11=smallest need)	TOTAL (Add self-assessment and team need ranks)	DEVELOPMENT PRIORITY (1=R with lowest TOTAL; 11=R with highestTOTAL)
Results	1	3	4	1-2-3 (tie)
Reality	9	4	13	5
Resources	6	9	15	6-7-8 (tie)
Rules	2	2	4	1-2-3 (tie)
Roles & Responsibilities	8	7	15	6-7-8 (tie)
Respectful Relationships	7	11	18	10-11- (tie)
Risk Taking	3	1	4	1-2-3 (tie)
Relentless Resolve	5	10	15	6-7-8 (tie)
Recovery	11	6	17	9
Recognition	4	5	9	4
Reflective Thinking	10	8	18	10-11- (tie)

Priority Assessment Form

When doing so, I adapt and use the reflective questions at the end of each chapter to assess each of the 11 R's. Then I prioritize. After that, I like to re-assess annually. In addition, I like to do quick, informal assessments whenever my team is struggling; it helps me pinpoint where I can provide more, better or different leadership. It's a diagnostic tool in that way. And it helps me be accountable because, when the going gets tough, I look both at my team and myself.

Before long, if you stick with this, you will be able to link past experiences with current leadership challenges and, as a result, diagnose problems on the fly. Even then, however, a quick review of the Leadership SOPs can help confirm your hunch and/or determine whether multiple factors may be at play. Also, the individual chapters are always helpful when it comes to framing your thoughts and planning how to attack a particular problem. To this day, I still reference these chapters, especially when the issues are more challenging.

Begin – The Rest is Easy

I've given you a lot to chew on:

- 11 Leadership SOPs (the R's), with distinct concepts and reflective questions;
- A suggestion that you assess yourself and team according to the SOPs;
- Encouragement to "try stuff" from the individual chapters and other sources;
- And a suggestion that you start a leadership journal.

Before all of that, I also introduced the "Zero to Something" philosophy, which is my leadership point of view –

the foundation for my entire approach. I want to conclude by making yet another suggestion – that you spend some time specifically thinking about the "Zero to Something" philosophy and relating it to your own leadership role. I believe you will find value, beyond the SOPs and assessments, by adopting this philosophy or adapting it to your own.

As you recall, "Zero to Something" is a mindset of methodically making progress toward your goals and ideals, confident that small, consistent progress will inevitably add up to big achievements. "Zero to Something" acknowledges that inertia and complacency are the natural enemies of all and that leaders overcome such tendencies by consciously exerting influence on destiny. It's a philosophy that says starting is the hardest part and that leaders are those willing to start, make progress, and then start again – over and over. The "Zero to Something" philosophy values discipline, structure, humility and personalization. It also says leadership begins in the mirror, requiring that we lead ourselves and then others.

Think about that last paragraph at work tomorrow. Think about it in your next meeting. Think about it when confronted with your next challenge or decision. See if it provides any clarity or direction. Revise it. Expand upon it. Reflect in your journal. At some point, hop on to *zerotosomething.com* and share your insights with others and me. I want to know how "Zero to Something" has been useful and applicable, and I want to learn from the ways you have adopted and adapted it.

Now, go. Reset the dial. You're at zero, en route to something. Next stop: something else. Eventually: something GREAT! ❖

Forms

	SELF ASSESSMENT (1=least developed; 11=most developed)	TEAM NEED (1=biggest need; 11=smallest need)	TOTAL (Add self-assessment and team need ranks)	DEVELOPMENT PRIORITY (1=R with lowest TOTAL; 11=R with highestTOTAL)
Results				
Reality				
Resources				
Rules				
Roles & Responsibilities				
Respectful Relationships				
Risk Taking				
Relentless Resolve				
Recovery				
Recognition				
Reflective Thinking				

Priority Assessment Form

Forms

	SELF ASSESSMENT (1=least developed; 11=most developed)	TEAM NEED (1=biggest need; 11=smallest need)	TOTAL (Add self-assessment and team need ranks)	DEVELOPMENT PRIORITY (1=R with lowest TOTAL; 11=R with highestTOTAL)
Results				
Reality				
Resources				
Rules				
Roles & Responsibilities				
Respectful Relationships				
Risk Taking				
Relentless Resolve				
Recovery				
Recognition				
Reflective Thinking				

Priority Assessment Form

Bibliography of Influences and References

Alcoholics Anonymous ("Big Book," 4th ed.) (2001). New York: AA World Services, Inc. Buckingham, M., & Coffman, C. (2000). *First, Break All the Rules: What The Worlds Greatest Managers Do Differently* (Rev. ed.). New York, NY: Simon & Schuster.

Carlson, R. (1996). *Don't Sweat the Small Stuff--and it's all small stuff.* New York, NY: Hyperion.

Carpenter, D. S., & Coyle, M. (2011). *Leadership Lessons: Dwight Eisenhower (an e-book).* http://newwordcity.com/nwcgrid/books/all/leadership-lessons-dwight-eisenhower/

Cashman, K. (2008). *Leadership from the Inside Out: Becoming a Leader for Life (2nd ed.).* San Francisco, CA: Berrett-Koehler Publishers.

Cleary, T. (Ed.). (1988). *The Art of War*: Sun Tzu. Boston, MA: Shambhala Publications.

Collins, J. C. (2001). *Good to Great: Why Some Companies Make the Leap... and Others Don't.* New York, NY: HarperBusiness.

Connors, R., Smith, T., & Hickman, C. (2004). *The Oz Principle (Rev. ed.).* New York, NY: Portfolio, a member of Penguin Group.

Covey, S. R. (1999). *The 7 Habits of Highly Effective People (Rev. ed.).* New York, NY: Simon & Schuster.

Dewey, J. (2007, orig. 1910). *How We Think*. Boston: Digireads.com.

Dodd, P., & Sundheim, D. (2005). *The 25 Best Time Management Tools and Techniques: How to Get More Done Without Driving Yourself Crazy*. Hoboken, NJ: John Wiley & Sons.

Forrester, D.P. (2011). *Consider: Harnessing the Power of Reflective Thinking*. New York: Palgrave Macmillan.

Gladwell, M. (2000). *The Tipping Point*. New York, NY: Little, Brown and Company.

Heath, C., & Heath, D. (2007). *Made to Stick: Why Some Ideas Survive and Others Die*. New York: Random House.

Hersey, P. (1985). *The Situational Leader*. New York: Warner Books.

Irvine, D., & Mosley, E. (2010). *Winning with a Culture of Recognition*. Dublin: Globoforce Limited.

Knight, B. (2013). *The Power of Negative Thinking: An Unconventional Approach to Achieving Positive Results*. Boston, MA: New Harvest, an imprint of Houghton Mifflin Harcourt.

Lencioni, P. M. (2002). *The Five Dysfunctions of a Team: A Leadership Fable*. San Francisco, CA: Jossey-Bass, an imprint of Wiley.

MacKay, H.B. (1988). *Swim with the Sharks Without Being Eaten Alive: Outsell, Outmanage, Outmotivate, and Outnegotiate Your Competition*. New York: Ivy Books.

Maxwell, J. C. (1999). *The 21 indispensable qualities of a leader : becoming the person others will want to follow: becoming the person others will want to follow*. Nashville, TN: Thomas Nelson.

Miller, J. G. (2004). *QBQ! The Question Behind the Question*. New York, NY: G.P. Putnam's Sons, a member of Penguin Group.

Nelson, B. (2005). *1001 Ways to Reward Employees.* New York: Workman Publishing Company.

Powell, C.L. (1996). *My American Journey.* New York: Random House.

Rath, T. (2007). *StrengthsFinder 2.0.* New York, NY: Gallup Press.

Rohn, J. (1996). *7 Strategies for Wealth & Happiness: Power Ideas from America's Foremost Business Philosopher (2nd ed.).* New York, NY: Harmony, an imprint of Random House's Crown Publishing Group.

Senge, P.M. (1990). *The Fifth Discipline: The Art & Practice of The Learning Organization.* New York: Doubleday/Currency.

Sundheim, D., & Schwartz, T. (2012). *Taking Smart Risks: How Sharp Leaders Win When Stakes Are High.* New York: McGraw Hill.

Tichy N. (1997). *The Leadership Engine: How winning companies build leaders at every level.* New York: HarperCollins.

The United States Army (2007). *Army Field Manual FM 22-100 (The U.S. Army Leadership Field Manual).* Boston, MA: Digireads.com.

Verzuh, E. (2011). *The Fast Forward MBA in Project Management (4th ed.).* New York: Wiley.

Welch, J, & Welch, S. (2005). *Winning.* New York: HarperCollins.

Willingham, R. (1999). *The People Principle: A Revolutionary Redefinition of Leadership.* London: Macmillan.

Acknowledgments

I would like to recognize the people who have inspired me and provided me with examples of what "Zero To Something" leadership can accomplish.

To my parents Arnold and Nobuko Strebe for your love, support and direction. To my brother Glenn, my sister Tori and my daughters Tori and Courtney for sharing your lives with me and providing so many opportunities to learn about myself and others. To my stepson Tanner, a young man wise beyond his years, for keeping me on my toes.

To the people I have led throughout my career, for the honor of doing so – this book would not exist without you. To Teresa Filleman and Amy Lenert for teaching me relentless resolve. To Jeremiah Gardner for helping me understand that sometimes it's OK to go with the flow. To Vince Robertson for his creative support.

To John Haydock, one of the best leaders I've known, for being a role model. To Frank Qiu and Ting Xu for exposing me to a truly amazing American success story that demonstrates how to take a simple idea from zero to something great. To John and Brittany Toler for drive and focus on results. To David Earle for reminding me that you don't have to be the loudest person in the room to be the most influential. To Kenny Ayscue and Terri Shiffer for showing me the powerful value of human resource leadership and development. To Alfred Schwan, Lenny Pippin, Greg Flack, Mark Dalrymple, Cal Brink and Michael B. Ziebell for extending career opportunities that allowed me to develop into a more well-rounded leader and person. To Connie Zaborowski for supporting me when I assumed responsibility of a large manufacturing plant with no prior experience in such an environment. To Sally Chial for giving me my first "real world" job after I retired from the military.

To Dale Bock, James Xu, Tere Eggleston, Melissa Barton, Dave Bickel, Frank Wood, Dana Pappas, Paul Abugattas, Rich Koval, Brianne Forst, Jennifer Kwiatkowski, Eve Chien, Beverly Fries, Grace Guo, and the Human Resources teams at Evergreen Enterprises and Plow and Hearth for their friendship and support during the past 3 years.

To Tim Francis who has been a great friend for over 30 years and one who has always been there for me.

To my wife Sigrid for her love, untiring support and ongoing reality checks from the beginning to the end of this undertaking.

Thank you all.

About the Authors

Arnie Strebe is the Chief Talent and Business Improvement Officer for Evergreen Enterprises and Plow & Hearth, both headquartered in Virginia. There, he leads the design, development and implementation of all people and performance improvement initiatives.

Arnie worked previously for Minnesota-based The Schwan Food Company, where as a member of the Senior Executive Development Program, he held operational assignments in sales and marketing, manufacturing, human resources, and learning and development. Among his achievements at Schwan was the founding of Schwan's University, an employee training and development organization that earned several national and international awards for excellence. Arnie also held senior leadership positions at URS Corporation, an international engineering firm, and the Minnesota Department of Transportation.

Arnie holds a master's degree in education. Prior to entering the business world, he enjoyed a successful career in the U.S. Army as an enlisted soldier and officer. On the personal front, Arnie keeps busy as a certified USA Triathlon coach and has completed many triathlons himself, including three Ironman events. He also provides other fitness-related coaching, as well as executive coaching, and says his personal mission is to help others succeed. Arnie lives with his wife, Sigrid, in Richmond, Va. He has two grown daughters, Tori and Courtney, and a stepson, Tanner.

Jeremiah Gardner is a public relations and communications professional for the nonprofit Hazelden Betty Ford Foundation, a world leader in addiction treatment and recovery services, headquartered in Minnesota. There, he also manages the organization's online social community and contributes to public advocacy efforts. Jeremiah also is a writer and producer for the independent documentary film, *Miracle Cures and the History of Addiction Treatment*, which remained in production as this book went to press.

As a former newsman and editor for The Associated Press, Jeremiah has been published in newspapers throughout the United States, including the Los Angeles Times, Washington Post and Chicago Tribune. More recently, he worked at The Schwan Food Company as a technical writer, multimedia specialist, curriculum writer, training manager and performance consultant, helping the business earn several awards for training and development excellence.

Away from the office, Jeremiah has written, performed and recorded with a number of music groups. He also is an active triathlete and marathoner. He holds bachelor's degrees in journalism and political science and a master's degree in addiction studies, and he is licensed in Minnesota as an alcohol and drug counselor. Jeremiah was once named outstanding graduate at The Fund for American Studies' Institute on Political Journalism at Georgetown University, and he also has completed additional graduate courses in business and law. He lives in the Minneapolis area with his wife, Jenny, and twin sons, Keegan and Jace.

Take the next step in your development with this workbook designed to help you put **Zero to Something** LEADERSHIP into action.

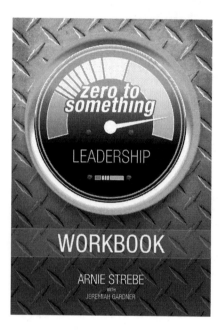

- The workbook reinforces the **Zero to Something** LEADERSHIP concepts in a condensed form for easy and frequent reference

- Designed for hands-on interaction, the workbook provides exercises, forms, reflective questions and a variety of other tools to help you apply **Zero to Something** LEADERSHIP lessons to your specific situations

- The workbook will help you begin to capture and refine your own unique approach to leadership for both personal and professional success

Whether leading yourself, a team, a project, an event or an organization, the Zero to Something LEADERSHIP workbook will be an invaluable resource on your way to accomplishing the results you desire!

Don't forget to download the companion WORKBOOK!

www.zerotosomething.com

Made in the USA
Lexington, KY
12 June 2019